CONRADIANA
A Journal of Joseph Conrad Studies

Volume 50   Winter 2018   Number 3

Dedicated to the Memory of J. Hillis Miller

FORUM: IN MEMORY OF J. HILLIS MILLER

Dedicated in Memory of J. Hillis Miller, 1928–2021   217
JOHN G. PETERS

J. Hillis Miller   219
JAKOB LOTHE

J. Hillis Miller   223
BYRON SANTANGELO

An Exemplary Reader: J. Hillis Miller on Criticism as Performance   227
NIDESH LAWTOO

ARTICLES

A Confucian Construction of Joseph Conrad's Sincerity   243
AN NING

Dark Borneo: Yong-Ping Li's Reworkings of *Heart of Darkness*
and *Lord Jim* in *The End of the River*   259
TUNG-AN WEI

The True Self as Social Solidarity in Conrad's *The Secret Sharer*
and *The Shadow-Line*   277
ERIK ROBB THOMPSON

REVIEW

NIDESH LAWTOO on *Reading Conrad* by J. Hillis Miller,
edited by John G. Peters and Jakob Lothe   299

Contributors   313

Dedicated to the Memory of J. Hillis Miller, 1928–2021

JOHN G. PETERS

I never personally met Joseph Hillis Miller, but I corresponded with him on a number of occasions. I first wrote to him while working on *Joseph Conrad's Critical Reception*. I had read his chapters on Conrad in his *Poets of Reality* previously, but it was only when I re-read these chapters in the context of other scholarship that was being published on Conrad during the mid-1960s that I realized just how unique his work on Conrad was for the time in which it was written. There was of course some fine work done during that period with the commentary on Conrad's politics by Eloise Knapp Hay and Avrom Fleishman, for example, but Hillis's work was completely different from anything else appearing at that time and anticipated work that would appear some ten or twenty years later. I was so struck by the originality of Hillis's work that I sent him a message to that effect, and our correspondence began from there. As I continued working on subsequent decades of commentary for my history of Conrad commentary, I was surprised at just how much work Hillis had done on Conrad. Although he never wrote a monograph on Conrad, his criticism on Conrad in *Poets of Reality, Fiction and Repetition*, and his essay on *Heart of Darkness* that appeared in the collection *Conrad Revisited* have been particularly influential, and other work on "The Secret Sharer," *Nostromo*, as well as other Conrad writings are of equal standing. It was at that point that I had the thought that if I was unaware just how much Hillis had written on Conrad that others were likely unaware as well and that it might be a good idea to collect together his writings on Conrad into a single volume. Thus began *Reading Conrad*, the collection that I co-edited with Jakob Lothe, reviewed by Nidesh Lawtoo in this volume. Hillis was very pleased with the idea and helped guide the project to its completion. Through this experience, I discovered just how kind and generous he was. As a luminary figure in literary studies, he might easily have been unapproachable or too engulfed in his own work to have time for others. I have known some prominent scholars who were that way, but Hillis was different. He seemed to take pleasure in supporting others, giving of his time and experience to benefit others. I am sorry not to have met him personally (he was unable to travel anymore by the time our friendship began), but I have greatly benefitted from his knowledge and generosity and will forever remember him fondly.

J. Hillis Miller

JAKOB LOTHE

J. Hillis Miller made very important contributions to critical trends as different as phenomenology, deconstruction, and narrative ethics. He also made a significant contribution to Conrad studies. Over the course of a career that lasted from the mid-1950s until 2020, Miller turned, and returned, to Conrad's fiction, reading, rereading, and discussing key texts in the light of theoretical developments to which he had himself contributed.

If Miller's strong and lasting interest in Conrad says something about the range of his critical interests, it also tells us something about the narrative sophistication and thematic richness of Conrad's fiction. When John G. Peters and I co-edited Miller's *Reading Conrad* (The Ohio State University Press, 2017), we were forcibly struck by Miller's demonstration of the ways in which Conrad's fiction responds to varying critical approaches. While Miller draws on aspects of phenomenology in his discussion of *The Secret Agent* in *Poets of Reality: Six Twentieth-Century Writers* (1965), an essay entitled "The Interpretation of *Lord Jim*" (1970) signals his critical move from phenomenology towards deconstruction. There is a link between this essay and his chapter on *Lord Jim* in *Fiction and Repetition: Seven English Novels* (1982). There is also a connection between both these discussions and narrative hermeneutics as represented by the German philosopher Hans-Georg Gadamer. In *Truth and Method*, first published in German as *Wahrheit und Methode* in 1960, Gadamer argues that not only do we as readers interpret the same text differently, but the text itself contains interpretative elements that influence the reader's interpretation. *Lord Jim* is an excellent example of such a text since the novel's characters and narrators give varying, in part conflicting, interpretations of the main character Jim. Miller's interpretation of these interpretations is thoughtful and thought-provoking.

While Miller's literary criticism is consistently textual in its orientation, his studies of Conrad reveal a growing interest in, and focus on, elements of context and history. To put this another way, he becomes increasingly interested in the way in which the fiction is framed. Thus, while in an essay on *Heart of Darkness* from 1985 he writes of the narrative of *Heart of Darkness* as a general or unspecified process of unveiling, his interpretation of the same literary text in an essay published in 2002 makes him consider *Heart of Darkness* as a critique of imperialism. Similarly, the essay "'Material Interests': *Nostromo* as a Critique of Global Capitalism" (2008) pays more attention to this novel's historical context than his earlier discussions of *Lord Jim*. This historical contextualizing is linked not just to crucial aspects of Conrad's time but also to the situation of the critic and his readers. To use a key concept from Gadamer's *Truth and Method*, Miller is acutely aware of his own *horizon*. For Gadamer, the reader's and the critic's horizon signal a kind of limitation, yet also suggest a critical possibility as the critic can say something about a literary text from his or her own perspective. Miller's studies of Conrad are a critically productive, and remarkably original, combination of his horizon as a reader, as a critic, and as a human being.

Miller's contribution to the project "Narrative Theory and Analysis" that I ran at the Centre for Advanced Study, Oslo, in 2005–06 proved invaluable. He wrote excellent chapters for the three books (all of them published by The Ohio State University Press) in which the project resulted: *Joseph Conrad: Voice, Sequence, History, Genre* (2008), *Franz Kafka: Narration, Rhetoric, and Reading* (2011), and *After Testimony: The Ethics and Aesthetics of Holocaust Narrative for the Future* (2012). While his chapter in *After Testimony* is linked to *The Conflagration of Community: Fiction before and after Auschwitz* (2011), his contribution to *Joseph Conrad* is related to, and forms part of the basis for, a long chapter on *Nostromo* in *Communities in Fiction* (2015). Entitled "Conrad's Colonial (Non)Community," and dedicated to the memory of Edward W. Said, this chapter is interestingly linked to Said's discussion of *Nostromo* in *Beginnings: Intention and Method* (1975).

Moreover, during the extended periods of time he spent in Oslo, Miller was the most generous colleague that anyone will come across. Always ready to listen to the other project participants' ideas, and consistently constructive and encouraging in his comments, Miller contributed significantly to the good working atmosphere of the research team. I remember that sometimes he would arrive in Oslo directly from the East because he had been giving lectures in China. These lectures, incidentally, provided the basis for yet another book, *An Innocent Abroad: Lectures in China* (2015).

I want to close these remarks in memory of Miller by drawing attention to two aspects of his work that are linked to his lasting interest in Conrad. The first of these is his contribution to narrative ethics. For Miller, ethics has a peculiar yet strong relation to narrative, and there is a connection between the ethical moment in the act of reading and the ethical moment in the act of writing. This ethical moment is linked to an understanding of ethics as a place where the contest of values is presented, not where it is resolved. Yet as Miller shows, perhaps most convincingly in *Communities in Fiction*, it does not follow that Conrad's fiction is not possessed of an ethical dimension.

The second aspect, whose importance has rightly been emphasized by my colleague Jeremy Hawthorn, is Miller's concern with the state of the academy in general and of literary studies in particular. This aspect, too, is associated with his interest in Conrad. When Hawthorn and I co-edited *Narrative Ethics* (2013), Miller contributed a chapter entitled, "Should We Read or Teach Literature Now?" After having reflected on the diminished role of the humanities in higher education, Miller turns to W.B. Yeats's "The Cold Heaven," listing fifteen "things that might need to be explained" to a young reader of the poem. These "things" turn out to be perceptive and thought-provoking comments on a complex poem that is challenging to read and teach. Miller's strong interest in pedagogy here blends into his lasting commitment to literary studies and vice versa. Given that this essay is inspired by Miller's "Should We Read *Heart of Darkness*?" (2002), his concern with the profession of literary studies is related to his reading of Conrad.

Miller's combined interest in narrative form and narrative ethics partly explains why he continued to read, reread, and write about Conrad. His work on this author is consonant with a key point he makes in the first chapter of *Fiction and Repetition*. Literary criticism, he writes, "is nothing if it is not philology, the love of words, the teaching of reading." If literature matters, and if literary studies matter, Conrad was, for Miller, one of those authors who demonstrates that this is the case. Moreover, if Miller's criticism helps to establish why literature matters, it also establishes, again and again, why literary criticism also matters. Miller's understanding of narrative fiction, including fiction's value for the individual as well as for the community, was exceptional. We will remain grateful for his significant contribution to Conrad studies.

J. Hillis Miller

BYRON SANTANGELO

J. Hillis Miller (1928–2021) joined a rare and inspiring flexibility of mind with a deep sense of responsibility to others and otherness. These traits were reflected in his formulation of the ethics of reading, which foregrounds the importance of bearing witness as faithfully as possible through the act of interpretation. At the same time, he argued, careful reading unveils the impossibility of coming to a final account, since each interpretation adds something new or different and reveals the need for still further explanation and testimony. Readers must humbly confront the impossibility of closure. In this sense, to generate a loyal remembrance of Miller requires a recognition that it will necessarily be partial.

Miller was one of the most influential critics and theorists of his time and has had a profound, often inaugural, impact on the ways Conrad has been read. As so many other tributes attest, he was also a generous and beloved teacher, mentor, and colleague. Indeed, from my vantage point as a former graduate student of Miller's and as a fellow scholar of Conrad, he lived by the principles laid out in *The Ethics of Reading*, which included not only an obligation to but also respect for the other—whether text, someone else, or oneself.

In 1986, Miller moved to the University of California, Irvine, where he was Distinguished Professor of English and Comparative Literature, and established UCI's reputation as a preeminent center for the study of literary theory. He was already a towering figure in Victorian and Modernist literary studies and, as a member of the Yale School, had profoundly shaped the direction of literary theory and critical practice. At the time, he was also the current president of the Modern Language Association, from which he would receive the Francis Andrew March Award for Distinguished Service to the Profession in 2001 and the MLA Lifetime Scholarly Achievement Award in 2005.

I was an aspiring Conradian when Miller arrived at Irvine, and *Poets of Reality* (1965), *Fiction and Repetition* (1981), and *Conrad Revisited* (1985) had transformed how I understood and read Conrad. His explication of *Lord Jim* had been especially formative with its foregrounding of the ethical drive for faithful testimony and interpretation and of the always uncertain, ultimately indeterminate, results.

Graduate students eagerly anticipated his arrival, and we quickly signed up for his seminar which was based on what was to be *Versions of Pygmalion*. The students in the course were nervous, and initially we sat quietly listening to his lectures emphasizing how prosopopoeia (personification) in Nathaniel Hawthorne and Henry James both drives us to unveil the truth behind figuration and reveals the impossibility of achieving final understanding. However, over time he put us all at ease with his humor and his responses to student questions and comments. Indeed, I was struck by his indefatigable generosity not only with his time and guidance but also in his receptivity to our ideas and scholarly endeavors—including when they diverged or were even critical of his own. (One brilliant, if brazen, student cleverly mocked deconstruction through a reading of a Walter Scott novel; Miller chuckled and also engaged seriously with the critique, even if the rest of the class was left aghast.) At the same time, through both his example and his subtle but probing questions, Miller pushed us to pay closer attention to textual detail and to be open to the resistance to closure such attention entailed. Before I took that class, I thought I knew how to read. However, as he demonstrated the raveling and unraveling of meaning through rhetorical analysis, and as he emphasized both the ethical imperative to make an account (no one can do the reading for you) and the impossibility of doing so, I came to appreciate the trickiness of reading as a practice and the impossibility of moving beyond it.

A number of years after I completed my PhD under Miller's supervision, I was reminded once again of his generosity and principled rigor when we participated in a conference in South Africa marking the centenary of *Heart of Darkness* for which he was the keynote speaker. For his address, he gave an initial version of what would become a chapter in *Others* (2001) entitled, "Should We Read *Heart of Darkness*?" He argues, on the one hand, that we must each read *Heart of Darkness* and make our own judgement regarding racist and colonialist representation in the text and, on the other hand, that Conrad's thoroughgoing irony skewers "the ideology of capitalist imperialism." The conference included a wide range of scholars in approach and age. Many were closely associated with postcolonial and African literary studies, and their papers often diverged sharply from Miller's conclusions. He was especially interested in these readings, most of them from younger scholars and, far from being dismissive, was frequently complementary and supportive. At the same time, his respectful engagement with others' interpretations, with their testimony, was made evident through his subtle questions and observations that would take conversations in unexpected directions. The conference was a collegial, and indeed festive, affair, and led to numerous new, generative collaborations and professional friendships. Miller's generous, collegial approach to others both reflected and facilitated the best aspects of this absorbing experience and its long-term impact. More generally, he continued—and continues—to be a model of ethical, humble engagement with text and world for untold numbers of us who read, were taught, collaborated with, and befriended him.

An Exemplary Reader: J. Hillis Miller on Criticism as Performance

NIDESH LAWTOO

The disappearance of J. Hillis Miller left a yawning void among the community of literacy critics and theorists around the world, but the traces of his admirable readings live on and remain to be followed up. Professor Miller was, in fact, a brilliant teacher, an inspiring scholar, a generous and cherished friend, and, last but not least, an exemplary reader of literary and theoretical texts. As a Victorianist by training who soon transgressed antiquarian disciplinary boundaries, he had a special philological interest in modernism in general and in Joseph Conrad in particular. As he explains in his Introduction to *Reading Conrad* (edited by John Peters and Jakob Lothe), when he was thirteen or so he accidentally found a copy of Conrad's *Typhoon* in his father's library that cast a lifelong spell on his imagination—a spell so long that it will lead him to end his career with a performative promise about *Typhoon*. Early on, then, Conrad stood out for J. Hillis Miller, occupying a privileged place in his distinguished intellectual trajectory—beginning, middle, and end.

One of the most influential critics and theorists of the twentieth and twenty-first centuries, J. Hillis Miller started reading fiction early. As he explains in his last interview, he "taught [him]self to read at the age of five" (Lawtoo, "Critic" 97) so he could read children's books like *Winnie the Pooh*, *The Swiss Family Robinson*, and *Alice in Wonderland*—a formative experience that eventually led to an impressive, exploratory, and inimitable career in literary study. After obtaining a PhD in English Literature from Harvard University in an intellectual environment that was "actively hostile to literary theory" (98), as he recalls, Miller's critical and theoretical work took off with his engagement with New Criticism and phenomenology at The Johns Hopkins University, where he befriended Georges Poulet and first encountered Jacques Derrida, continued at Yale where he became an influential advocate of the "Yale School of Deconstruction" along with Derrida, Paul de Man, and Geoffrey Hartman, and culminated at the University of California, Irvine, where he contributed to the ethical turn by developing untimely readings on the importance of literature, reading, and community. After his retirement as Distinguished Research Professor Emeritus in 2002, Miller continued to write numerous books. In his

FIGURE 1: J. Hillis Miller's home on Deer Isle, Maine, *The Critic as Mime* (2018).

final years, he was increasingly concerned with the digital turn and climate change in the Anthropocene, writing from his visionary tower in his private home on Deer Isle, Maine, overseeing the Atlantic Ocean.

Since the 1960s, in sum, J. Hillis Miller inspired a chain of readers that reaches well into the present. He sadly passed away on February 7, 2021, at the venerable age of 92. Still, the art of reading he practiced in his writings is here to stay, its shape the same—a model for anyone looking for exemplary readers in the present and future centuries.

For these and other reasons, Miller was at the top of my list of intellectual models I wanted to interview for a transdisciplinary European Research Council project titled *Homo Mimeticus: Theory and Criticism*. The goal of this project is to reframe the ancient concept of "mimesis," which tends to be restricted to realistic representation, by focusing on the performative, affective, and embodied properties of *homo mimeticus* constitutive of what we started calling the "mimetic turn."[1] As a critic and theorist who spent his career challenging the view that literature simply represents a pre-existing referential reality, Miller was a natural ally for the mimetic turn. The interview, titled "The Critic and the Mime," turned out to be double in the end. Mimesis *oblige*, Miller and I had agreed on publishing a written version that would then be followed by a filmed, or cinematic, version. In a deconstructive irony that characterized his distinctive signature, the written (printed) version came thus "first" in the sense that we finalized it in the spring of 2018, whereas the oral (filmed) version came "second" as we shot it in the fall of 2018 on Labor Day (September 6).[2] The latter was intended as a cinematic shadow, or phantom, to the written traces we had already left behind but had not appeared in print as yet when we started filming. This is perhaps an implicit indication that new media that redouble and supplement the experience of writing continue to destabilize the fraught distinction between "original" and "copy" internal to the "orality/writing" binary. Post-literary media deserve equal critical attention in an increasingly digitized age, a point Miller stressed in the written interview as well, as he recognized that "the new digital media are taking over from literature" (Lawtoo, "Critic" 115). Already at the dawn of the twenty-first century, he remarked that "Conrad came toward the end of the epoch of literature" (Miller, "Foreword" 9). And he adds, not without irony, "If Conrad were around today he would probably be writing movie or television scripts, or programming computer games" (9). This does not mean that his fictions no longer deserve to be read closely. Quite the contrary, as we shall see.

On a more personal level, it is because I wanted to meet in person the exemplary reader of texts, be they literary or post-literary, who had played such a decisive role in my choice of embarking on a literary and philosophical career in the 1990s—leading me to aspire not so much to a secure job, let alone salary, but to become a "reader"—that, on September 6, 2018, I found myself driving from Boston up to Deer Isle, Maine, where Miller had kindly invited me to shoot the cinematic redux of the interview. Having reached Portland (Maine, not its better-known double in Oregon), I took the slower, more exploratory route along the coast I had seen on Google Maps. The experience of driving through towns with unoriginal names (Camden, Lincolnville, Belfast . . .) was largely compensated by scenic nautical views of the Atlantic that inevitably called Conrad to mind.

FIGURE 2: On the road to Deer Isle, Maine, *The Critic as Mime*.

FIGURE 3: Arrival on Deer Isle, Maine, *The Critic as Mime*.

The journey felt like travelling back in time. Not quite to the "earliest beginnings of the world," as Marlow famously puts it in *Heart of Darkness* (33), but to the beginning of my personal fascination with the art of reading. I had fallen under its spell via the mediation of teachers who had been students and friends of Hillis in the 1970s. At two removes, then, I was mimetically indebted to the legendary "Deconstructive Angel" (Abrams) or "Critic as Host" (Miller), to quote two influential essays at the heart of the theory wars.[3] Such reading performances trained me in the practice of "rumination" (Nietzsche, *Genealogy* 10) advocated well before by that other untimely philologist *qua* reader par excellence that is Friedrich Nietzsche, and who equally served as my main source of inspiration.

Personal genealogies aside, both versions of the interview turned out to be amongst Hillis's last statements—probably the very last—on the importance of reading in the strong rhetorical or philological sense: a warning to slow down in an age haunted by increasingly fast new media simulations, rising (new) fascist threats, and rapid climate change in the age of the Anthropocene. Perhaps these doubling interviews even served as a sort of testament on reading, certainly a testimony, in the sense that Hillis took the occasion of this encounter to retrace the twists and turns in the labyrinth of his long and influential career: from phenomenology to the linguistic turn, the ethical turn to the digital turn to the environmental turn, all of which, we agreed, are entangled in a "mimetic turn or re-*turn* of mimesis" (Lawtoo, "Critic" 94), which is not a simple return to realism but generates performative effects and affects instead.

In what follows, I would like to show how this mimetic turn is performatively at play in Miller's last reflections on Joseph Conrad. I already stated in the review of *Reading Conrad* included in this special issue of *Conradiana* that reading, in the strong Nietzschean sense that Miller practiced it throughout his career, calls for a patient performative practice. As he puts it in one of his numerous essays on *Heart of Darkness*, "'No one can do your reading for you'" (Miller, "Should We Read" 463). A tribute to Miller's career, then, also entails an implicit performative address: "Do your own reading. Don't wait for me to do it for you." The loss of Miller's passing is thus not balanced but rather supplemented by the ethical imperative to further the practice of rhetorical reading he initiated so many of us into in the first place. In what follows, I will thus focus on reading, as best as I can, some examples taken from Miller's two last texts on Conrad: his brief introduction to *Reading Conrad*, titled "Conrad and Me,"[4] and the mirroring companion piece, titled "What Happens When I Read Conrad." They both illustrate the performative powers at play in his exemplary practice of reading constitutive of the mimetic turn.

Examples are never innocent, for they serve as models. They are thus mimetic in a sense that is already plural. First, examples provide particular manifestations of a kind that illustrate more general principles, or laws; in this concrete case, as Miller's last Conradian titles suggest, principles concerning his experience in reading "Conrad." Second, examples are also mimetic in the sense that they can be performed, or "mimed," as the titles of both our written and cinematic interviews echo. Third, and at one additional remove, examples can be furthered copied, or imitated via a form of active or performative mimesis, as the reference to the "exemplary reader" in this essay's title implies. I note that Miller himself was very fond of examples, if only because they provided him with the textual evidence to perform his readings in the first place. "I urge you to give me some examples" (Lawtoo, "Critic" 110), he told me in one of the few moments in our dialogue where we happened to have a friendly disagreement. I could not have agreed more with this performative imperative!

I now turn to the first example from "Conrad and Me" that opens *Reading Conrad*. Despite its brevity, it frames the totality of Miller's writings on Conrad, which he revisits at the end of his career. It thus casts a retrospective light on all the other readings of Conrad's tales that punctuate his career, from the 1960s to the present. This short introduction, as anticipated, has a double life, for Hillis reworked it for a conference held in New York in 2017 he attended virtually, that is, as a simulacrum on a screen.

The talk was subsequently published in a special issue of *Conradiana* titled "Conradian Crosscurrents" (edited by Christopher GoGwilt, Ellen Burton

FIGURE 4: J. Hillis Miller, "Conradian Crosscurrents," New York, 2017.

Harrington, and Nidesh Lawtoo). His essay ended with an enticing promise, "My time is up, however, and I must stop, though with a promise (another speech act) that I'll try to write an essay on what happens when I read [present] or read [past] *Typhoon*" ("What Happens" 284). In a subsequent, amplified echo, when I last saw Hillis in 2018 he was at work on a manuscript provisionally titled, *What Happens When I Read, Watch, or Play* (Lawtoo, "Critic" 116). I imagine the section on reading would have included a piece on *Typhoon* but, although we subsequently discussed plans to collaborate on this book—I was supposed to join forces on the "Watch" and "Play" section, though far from a proficient player of videogames myself—I do not know if Miller could keep that promise. He knew his time was short; he said he would "try." Still, as he reminds us, a promise is a performative "speech act." If it works for both "present" and "past" readings, once spoken, written, or, as in this case, both, it continues to address readers in the future as well. Whether it can generate performative speech acts that can certainly not replace the "original" promise, far from it, but can perhaps try, no doubt inadequately, to echo or supplement it, via what is basically an endnote to Miller's texts, is what we now turn to find out.

As the first "original" title ("Conrad and Me") of Miller's last meditation on the author of *Typhoon* suggests, this prefatory essay provides an indeterminate open-ended frame that is as much about Conrad as it is about Miller. As such, it introduces destabilizing doubling effects between autobiography and fiction that are not without broader mirroring reflections between the literary author and the literary critic more generally, casting an indirect light on all the essays in *Reading Conrad* it frames as well. This introductory frame is deceptively simple because of its autobiographical nature, colloquial tone, almost oral or spoken narrative voice, and allegorical brevity. Yet, one should not be deceived. Readers of Miller will have learned to recognize that in a critical/theoretical repetition with a difference, it performs, rather than simply representing, a narrative form, or genre, that is at the palpitating heart of Miller's experience of reading Conrad, is central to *Reading Conrad*, and sheds a twice-reflected light on the chapters that surround it: namely, the form of the parable. As Miller reminds us in what is arguably one of his most influential essays on Conrad, "Heart of Darkness *Revisited*," "The distinctive feature of the parable, whether sacred or secular, is the use of a realistic story . . . to express another reality or truth not otherwise expressible" (74). The formal choice to frame *Reading Conrad* with a parabolic tale is, of course, not innocent. The parable is, in fact, *the* literary form par excellence Miller convokes to describe the narrative style of Conrad's most famous tale in general; he convokes it to account for the "twice-refracted" reflections of the moon/halo parable the frame narrator himself uses to introduce Marlow's tale, in particular (Miller, "*Heart*" 41–43). It is perhaps no accident, then, that at yet an additional remove—at three removes, so to speak—Miller also relies on a parabolic form mediated in an oral tone to go outside the "hosting" literary text and shed light on the critic's own personal relation to Conrad. He does so, appropriately, in a doubling-realistic-autobiographical-parabolic piece simply titled, "Conrad and Me."

What Miller's parable urges future readers to trace is not so simple, though. It is nothing less and nothing more than the very "origins" of his own interests in Conrad's tales. And if typical uses of the parable might be "realistic" and thus mimetic in the straightforward sense of representational, the least one can say of Miller is that, not unlike Marlow, he "was not typical" (Conrad, *Heart* 5). Hence, Miller, who, by the way, considered "the language of criticism . . . continuous with the language of criticism" ("Host" 443), does not use his parable to point to a single meaning that can be cracked open, like a nut. Instead, he uses this parabolic/critical language to generate complex and destabilizing mirroring effects between fiction and reality, critic and host, that require reading in the strong, performative, and thus rhetorical sense to be traced.

As anticipated in my framing introduction, Miller narrates how he discovered *Typhoon* in his father's library "by accident" ("Conrad" 2) in his youth. His father would have been familiar with parables as well, especially sacred and Biblical ones. A "Southern Baptist minister" (2) with a strong interest in education, Miller tells us that his father had written a dissertation titled, *The Practice of Public Prayer*. Half-jokingly, he makes the serious, archival-minded, perhaps even pious scholar wonder: could *Typhoon* have been used as a secondary source for his father's theological dissertation, before turning into the son's primary object of literary investigation? "There is scholarship for you—mine, at least!" (3), Miller adds, in a characteristically Conradian ironic mood. Actually, these are the traces of what he subsequently calls a "false lead," for there is no trace of Conrad's novel in his father's dissertation, just as there is no evidence of public prayers in *Typhoon*. "Great hypothesis, but no evidence to support it" (3), he ironically adds. Miller's parable, then, entails a cautionary tale. He reminds readers before they embark on *Reading Conrad* of what is arguably *the* fundamental intrinsic principles of rhetorical reading: namely, that literary scholars need textually based interpretations on top of historical facts to support their critical hypotheses. This secular parable, we already begin to see, may refer mimetically to the referential reality of Miller's biographical life outside the text; yet, for the "critic as host," reading Conrad always already starts with the "experience" of reading the words inside the text. "There is a rhetorical principle for you—read at least!" I see him implying with his characteristic smile, between the lines.

For J. Hillis Miller and those trained in the tradition of rhetorical or philological reading, mimetic references to the world outside the text always need to be supplemented by close rhetorical attention to the words inside the text. This also means that mimesis, even in a realistic parable, is always double-faced, for it looks both inside and outside, generating mirroring destabilizing effects between linguistic signs and referential realities that were once constitutive of the linguistic turn and now, with a material supplement we shall soon consider, are constitutive of the mimetic turn as well.

Internal to "Conrad and Me," Miller supplements an interesting revelation concerning proper, or improper, names that may appear simply accidental and autobiographical but, on a closer look, continue to shed an indirect critical light on the "sacred or secular" performative powers of Miller's parable. As he explains, his own marker of personal identity (from Latin, *identitas*, the same), namely his name, was not singular or original but was double and reproductive. His father's name was, in fact, also J. Hillis Miller. This doubling leads J. Hillis Miller to specify: "My father is the real J. Hillis Miller. I am J. Hillis Miller Jr." (2). This mirroring phrase is revelatory of a mimetic sameness, yet J. Hillis Miller introduces a mimetic difference. If Jr. is one of those signifiers that has no signification without its counterpart, "Sr.," the binary also makes clear who comes first and who comes second, who is the "original," so to speak, and who is the "copy." The binary is not flattering. It relegates one of the best critics and theorists of the past half century to a secondary ontological position, to adopt Platonic categories. And yet, the ironic tone of the passage constitutive of its rhetoric might also indicate that the hierarchy of this binary is not vertical and stabilizing, positing the figure of the father over and against the son but, rather, horizontal, subversive, and playful. "J. Hillis Miller Jr." is, in fact, also implicitly blurring the distinction between "*the real* J. Hillis Miller" and—as the binary counterpart implies—the "fictional" one. In such a playful inversion there might already be a serious lesson about mimesis for readers to see from the interplay between mirroring words. Miller was always on the side of fiction, after all. Which also means that he sided with linguistic traces, copies, or simulacra that are secular in nature, which he often posited over and against "origins," ideals, and theological principles that are "sacred" in principle—yet rest on parabolic fictions as well.

In the end, then, the experience that mattered for the young Miller as he discovered *Typhoon* in his father's library was, of course, a secular but not less inspiring reading experience. He ironically comments that, while in the midst of the typhoon that gives the tale its title, the first mate of the *Nan-Shan*, Jukes, is thrown across the deck by a "great wall of water." Conrad specifies: "he kept on repeating mentally, with the utmost precipitation, the words: 'My God! My God! My God! My God!" (qtd. in Miller, "Conrad" 3). Within the tale, this is a mimetic repetition with performative aspirations whose dramatic intention is arguably to convoke the presence of God so as to stop the wall of water. It might approximate what believers call a prayer. But Miller ironically comments that Juke repeating this phrase "mentally" would not have been audible to Captain MacWhirr, "even if he had spoken aloud, so tremendous is the noise" (3). Whether this invocation is heard by God is doubtful within the tale, thus it is only accessible to the reader. No matter how hard one looks, there is, indeed, no sacred redeeming principle in Conrad's materialist and secular universe. At one remove, on the side of criticism, this may as well apply to Miller's parable as well.

As we enter deeper in the age of the Anthropocene, it is difficult not to see evidence that the threats of "walls of water" become more manifest every year generating typhoons at an unprecedented speed. Living on an island, literally a few steps away from the water, Miller was painfully aware of a referential environmental reality that did not receive enough attention in the past century (including by rhetorical critics), but that requires full critical attention in the present century. He makes this critical point in response to the collection of essays included in his last *Conradiana* article, writing, "I wish more attention had been paid here and there to the current context of reading, teaching, and writing about Conrad. I mean the rapidly accelerating species-destroying climate change within which we all live today" ("What Happens" 280). And he adds: "Conrad's fiction dramatizes the behavior that has ultimately led, no doubt unintentionally, to climate change" (280). If deconstruction was traditionally suspicious of referential realities and Miller even faults his major model, Jacques Derrida, for devoting a "very minor" place in work to climate change (Lawtoo, "Critic"), the Anthropocene looms large in Miller's last writings. As he warns readers in the company of Tom Cohen and Claire Colebrook (and echoing Nietzsche), we must be ready to face the "twilight of the idols" and take ethical responsibility to curb climate change before it is too late (and it's already very, perhaps too, late). As Miller puts it in 2016:

> We are experiencing global climate change that may soon make the species *Homo sapiens* extinct, after putting our coasts and coastal cities under water (New York City, for example, not to speak of Florida and my coastal home on Deer Isle, Maine). (Cohen, Colebrook, and Miller, 127)

This is an (un)timely warning that brings us back to the "catastrophic disturbance of the atmosphere" (20) Conrad had already registered in *Typhoon*. It is a warning that finds an echo in the present author's call to "inaugurate a reading of Conrad in the age of the Anthropocene" so as to face "catastrophes" to come.[5] That these catastrophes include what I called, also in 2016, "the shadow of epidemics [that] looms large on the horizon" (Lawtoo, *Shadow* 43, 92) only lends empirical justification to these joint untimely warnings.

What we can learn from *Typhoon*, among other things, is that praying won't be of much help in facing the spiraling and amplifying human/nonhuman feedback loops internal to the environmental catastrophes to come that humans, with different degrees of responsibility, have set in motion. Anthropocentric models, just like theocentric models, need to be revisited, and this revisiting is at play in Miller's final reflections. Repeated over time, Miller's imaginative youthful experience of going through the storm on the *Nan-Shan* was not theological but literary, not transcendent but purely immanent, not sacred but secular, not spellbound by human actions alone but by nonhuman forces as well. Above all, this hypnotic spell was induced by the performative effect of reading the words printed on the pages of *Typhoon*. For Miller, this reading experience was indeed nothing less than "the beginning of the lifelong fascination with Conrad's fictions" (3). It led to all those exemplary essays assembled in *Reading Conrad*.

And yet, as these remarks on the Anthropocene suggest, this does not mean that the binary between fiction and reality, imaginative experience and embodied experience, being inside the text and being outside the text, are watertight. Far from it. Miller's parable specifies that at one remove, on the side of reality, the experience of reading *Typhoon* also generated embodied effects that are

FIGURE 5A: *The First Sail: J. Hillis Miller: A Film Book.*

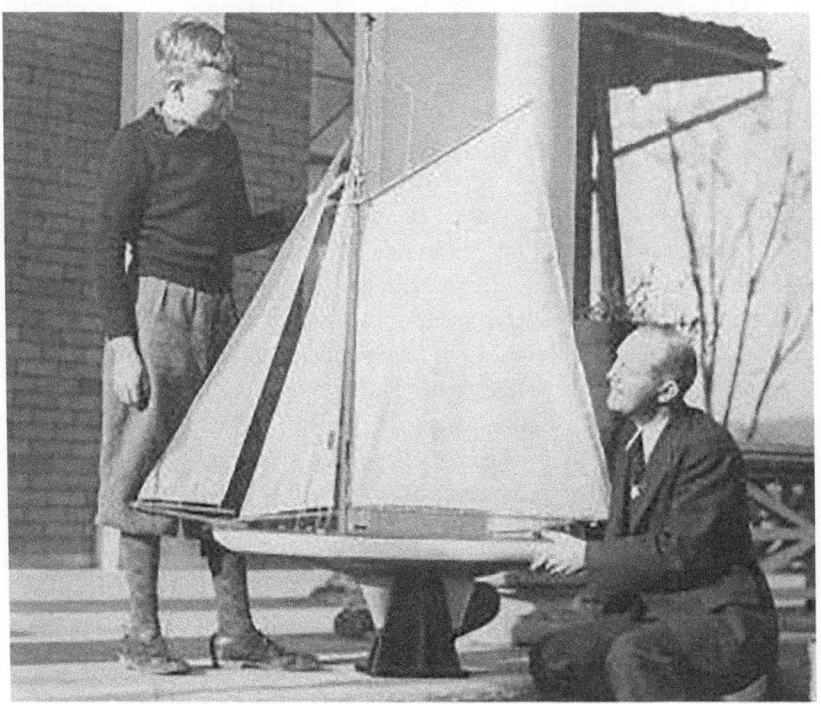

FIGURE 5B: J. Hillis Miller sailing, Deer Isle, *The First Sail.*

not without mimetic connections with the tale he was reading. As Miller puts it, it was also the beginning of his "lifelong love of small boat sailing, something I still do at the age of eighty-seven" (3).

The passage is worth quoting in full:

> My admiration for Conrad's work may also have something to do with my lifelong love of small boat sailing, something I still do at the age of eighty-seven, just as I still read Conrad with delight and with abiding admiration for his genius at creating imaginary worlds on the basis of his experiences and, in the case of *Nostromo* and some others, on the basis of his reading too. (3)

At the "origins" of Miller's fascination with Conrad and, by extension, imaginative literature more generally, we do not find a clear-cut opposition between fiction and reality, literary practices and bodily practices, the signs inside the text and the world outside, reading and sailing. On the contrary, what was true for Conrad's fictional tales is equally true, in different ways, for Miller's critical parable: the two co-exist side by side on the mirror of the sea, generating a mimetic interplay that implicates both critic and host in nautical experiences that are partially shared [*partagiées*] and that gave birth to Conrad's fictional tales in the first place.

With respect to his own relation with Conrad, Miller is cautious to leave the space between reading fiction and sailing his boat open, as he says that the former "may have something to do" with the latter. What is certain is that at the end of his parable Miller does not posit stable hierarchical binaries that privilege one pole over the other. Thus, he concludes "Conrad and Me" with what Nietzsche would call a "dangerous perhaps" (*Beyond* 34), for it introduces a fundamental wavering, hesitation, or oscillation in Miller's (anti-)mimetic art of reading. After having developed the anti-mimetic hypothesis that gives fiction priority over reality, in the sense that reading *Typhoon* may have been the beginning of his lifelong fascination with sailing, he inverts perspectives one last time. Thus, he notes that the experience of sailing itself actually "predates" and, perhaps, in-*forms* (gives form to), in mysterious, non-referential, yet nonetheless performative ways, the art of what he calls his "reading." His confessional parable ends, in fact, with the following supplementary mirroring inversion of perspectives: "Or perhaps it is the other way round, since my interest in sailing, encouraged by my father, predates my reading of *Typhoon*" (3).

What gives? At the end of the doubling and redoubling at play in this parabolic account of "Conrad and Me," "I," among a chain of readers, find myself unable to fix a stable "origin" across the fiction/reality divide to firmly anchor my reading of *Reading Conrad*. Perhaps this "origin" could be *both* inside the text *and*, as Miller's concluding phrase suggests, outside the text—that is, *hors-texte*. What I can perhaps say is that rhetorical critics and mimetic theorists benefit from joining forces in the age of the Anthropocene, joining forces with different perspectives (feminist, decolonial, new materialist, environmental, among other perspectives already internal to *homo mimeticus*) to read the signs of catastrophic shadows that loom larger than ever over the horizon—in order to see them coming and, with luck, affirm survival for generations to come.

In the end of reading "Conrad and Me" we might ask: who, then, is the *subject* of such mimetic "experiences" (3) (etymologically, *ex-perience* originally means to traverse, but also "sea passage"[6])? And *who* is actually reading here? J. Hillis Miller is, of course, at the singular-plural "origin" of *Reading Conrad* since he wrote all those splendid essays. But at the same time, in a mirroring inversion of perspectives in which the relation between reader and writer, critic and host, is destabilized, Miller had already urged his readers to consider that Conrad, the author of *Nostromo*, was not only drawing on his sailing experiences; he was drawing on reading experiences too, for Miller specifies Conrad was "reading too" (3). In a characteristic move, the critic as host does not stabilize this destabilizing interplay between reading and writing, reality and fiction, critic and host. Instead, he performatively encourages future readers of *Reading Conrad* to *both* read *and* experience this fascinating play on words. This is not only an effective rhetorical conclusion for one of the most significant books on Conrad to appear at what Miller calls "the end of Western-styled literature" (100).

FIGURE 6: J. Hillis Miller's library, Deer Isle, *The Critic as Mime*.

It is also a wonderfully indeterminate performative beginning for new generations of readers who are encouraged to extend the experience of reading to ruminate new visual media as well.[7]

Whether J. Hillis Miller's reading performance will continue to inspire new generations of readers to transfer the skills of rhetorical reading to face the mountainous challenges of the twenty-first century remains to be seen. If Conrad continues to remain one of us at the end of the age of literature, it is also because the catastrophes he dramatized in tales like *Typhoon* will continue to haunt all of us in the age of the Anthropocene. Perhaps then in an age in which the art of reading such tales is speedily disappearing, Miller's exemplary writings will continue to provide admirable models for readers to come. Such models, it should be clear by now, cannot be simply copied, or passively reproduced. I tried to show that with some training, patience, and above all, in the right company, interpretations can perhaps be re-*produced* (produced again), via performative mimetic principles vital to keeping the practice of reading as an art alive.

ACKNOWLEDGMENTS

I would like to thank J. Hillis Miller, one last time, for the inspiring nature of his work and for taking the time to discuss the art of reading with me while hosting me on Deer Isle. That he was ultimately happy with both written and filmed versions of the interview (in one of his last emails he wrote, with characteristic generosity: "Thank you, thank you for doing this") far exceeded my "original" youthful aspirations. This project has received funding from the European Research Council (ERC) under the European Union's Horizon 2020 research and innovation programme (grant agreement n°716181).

NOTES

1. Joseph Conrad occupies a privileged role in the mimetic turn internal to a trilogy of books (see Lawtoo, *Conrad's Heart*; Lawtoo, *Phantom* 85–141; Lawtoo, *Conrad*) whose main insights are condensed in Lawtoo, "Mimetic Turn." The *re*-turn of mimesis internal to *homo mimeticus* is now larger in disciplinary critical and theoretical scope as it moves from modernism to film, philosophy to politics and includes collaborations with continental philosophers (Jean-Luc Nancy), political theorists (William Connolly and Jane Bennett), anthropologists (Christoph Wulf), and feminist theorists (Adriana Cavarero), among others. See http://www.homomimeticus.eu/. Accessed 23 August 2021.

2. See https://www.youtube.com/watch?v=oM-TSY2nX-4. Accessed 20 August 2021.

3. See Abrams, and Miller, "Critic as Host."

4. For a more detailed discussion, see Peters and Lothe, "Foreword," and Lawtoo, "Reading."

5. For a reading of *Typhoon* that starts taking Conrad studies in the Anthropocene, see also, Lawtoo, *Conrad* xxxi–xxxiv, 41–48; and the essays in Schneider-Rebozo, McCarthy, and Peters, eds.

6. Thinking of the *Odyssey*, but with Conrad not too far from his preoccupations, Philippe Lacoue-Labarthe specifies that the term "experience is a nautical term": "ex-perience: to traverse, in the maritime sense of a sea passage [*traversee maritime*]" (110; my translation). For Miller's response to Lacoue-Labarthe's reading of Conrad, see Miller, "Revisiting."

7. The reader who carefully attended to the words that preceded might wonder: why does reading still matter in a world in which literature has lost its power of influence to new digital media? To which Miller replies to readers in the digital age that "literature matters most for us if it is read for today, and read rhetorically, to some degree as training in ways to spot lies, ideological distortions, and hidden political agendas such as surround us on all sides in the media these days" (*Thinking Literature* 54). Moreover, in a chapter titled "Should We Read or Teach Literature Now" that echoes and amplifies one of his Conrad essays, he adds that students and adults alike "might benefit from courses that would teach them how to tell truth from falsehood on Internet postings" (*Thinking Literature* 196). For Miller's latest position on new media, from cinema to videogames, see "Differences," and Miller, Callus, and Corby.

WORKS CITED

Abrams, M. H. "The Deconstructive Angel." *Critical Inquiry*, vol. 3, no. 3, 1977, pp. 425–38.
Cohen, Tom, Claire Colebrook, and J. Hillis Miller. *Twilight of the Anthropocene Idols*, Open Humanities Press, 2016.
Conrad, Joseph. *Heart of Darkness*. 5th ed., edited by Paul B. Armstrong, W.W. Norton, 2017.
———. *Typhoon and Other Stories*. Doubleday, 1925.
Kujundzic, Dragan. *The First Sail: J. Hillis Miller*, 2011.
Lacoue-Labarthe, Philippe. *La Réponse d'Ulysse: Et autres textes sur L'Occident*, edited by Aristide Bianchi and Leonid Kharlamov, Lignes/Imec, 2012.
Lawtoo, Nidesh, ed. *Conrad's Heart of Darkness and Contemporary Thought: Revisiting the Horror with Lacoue-Labarthe*. Bloomsbury, 2012.
Lawtoo, Nidesh. "Conrad's Mimetic Turn," *Conradiana*, vol. 48, nos. 2-3, 2016, pp. 129–42.
———. *Conrad's Shadow: Catastrophe, Mimesis, Theory*. Michigan State University Press, 2016.
———. "The Critic and the Mime: J. Hillis Miller in Dialogue with Nidesh Lawtoo," *Minnesota Review*, no. 95, 2020, pp. 93–119.
———. HOM Videos ERC Project Homo Mimeticus. "HOM Videos, ep. 2, The Critic as Mime: J. Hillis Miller." YouTube, uploaded by HOM Videos ERC Project Homo Mimeticus, May 23, 2019, https://www.youtube.com/watch?v=oM-TSY2nX-4&t=120s.
———. *The Phantom of the Ego: Modernism and the Mimetic Unconscious*. Michigan State University Press, 2013.

———. "Reading *Reading Conrad*." *Conradiana*, vol. 50, no. 3, 2018, pp. 299–311.

Miller, Hillis, J. "The Critic as Host." *Critical Inquiry*, vol. 3, no. 3, 1977, pp. 439–47.

———. "Differences in the Discipline of Literary Studies." *Symplokē*, vol. 25, nos. 1–2, 2017, pp. 529–34.

———. "Foreword." *Conrad in the Twenty-First Century: Contemporary Approaches and Perspectives*, edited by Carola Kaplan, Peter Mallios, and Andrea White, Routledge, 2015, pp. 1–14.

———. "*Heart of Darkness* Revisited." *Heart of Darkness and Contemporary Thought: Revisiting the Horror in the Company of Lacoue-Labarthe*, edited by Nidesh Lawtoo, Bloomsbury, 2012, pp. 39–54.

———. *Reading Conrad*. Edited by John G. Peters and Jakob Lothe, The Ohio State University Press, 2017.

———. "Revisiting '*Heart of Darkness* Revisited' (in the Company of Philippe Lacoue-Labarthe)." *Heart of Darkness and Contemporary Thought: Revisiting the Horror in the Company of Lacoue-Labarthe*, edited by Nidesh Lawtoo, Bloomsbury, 2012, pp. 13–35.

———. "Should We Read *Heart of Darkness*?" in Joseph Conrad, *Heart of Darkness*, 4th ed., edited by Paul B. Armstrong, W.W. Norton, 2006, pp. 463–73.

———. "What Happens When I Read Conrad?" *Conradiana*, vol. 48, nos. 2–3, 2016, pp. 279–85.

Miller, Hillis, J., and Ranjan Gosh. *Thinking Literature Across Continents*. Duke University Press, 2016, pp. 45–68.

Miller, Hillis, J., Ivan Callus, and James Corby. "The *CounterText* Interview: J. Hillis Miller." *CounterText*, vol. 4, no. 1, 2018, pp. 1–8.

Nietzsche, Friedrich. *Beyond Good and Evil*. Translated by R. J. Hollingdale, Penguin Books, 2003.

———. *The Genealogy of Morals*. Translated by Douglas Smith, Oxford University Press, 1996.

A Confucian Construction of Joseph Conrad's Sincerity

AN NING

SHANTOU UNIVERSITY

Keywords: Joseph Conrad, sincerity, *Cheng*, Confucianism, human solidarity, the meaning of being

ABSTRACT

This essay starts from a question: Why are Conrad's works so enduring and far reaching? A basic Confucian concept, *Cheng* (诚, sincerity), seems to offer a ready answer to this question. According to *The Doctrine of the Mean* (中庸, one of *The Four Books*), "entire sincerity is ceaseless," meaning if a person possesses absolute sincerity, his influence will be long lasting and far reaching. This essay demonstrates that sincerity is one of Conrad's essential personal traits, which serves as a guiding principle in his treatment of human relationships and his aesthetic handling of art. First it attempts to remove the two doubts hanging over Conrad's sincerity as an author and as a friend—his obscurity and his duplicity. It then exposes deeper affinities between Conrad's sincerity and the Confucian *Cheng*, to see how they tackle the following questions: How is sincerity defined? What is the role of sincerity in the universe? And how important is sincerity for human relationships? Finally, this essay concludes that sincerity, for Conrad, means singleness of mind; it is the foundation of artistic endeavor and forms the basis of human solidarity, through which one achieves the meaning of being.

Roland Barthes argues that reading "is always the same question: *What is it for me?*" (13) As a Chinese reader with a deep-rooted Confucian background,[1] I have been asking myself: What is Conrad for me? According to reader-response critics, "[t]he finding of meanings involves both the author's text and what the reader brings to it" (Rosenblatt 14). Interestingly, Conrad anticipates this critical trend. For instance, he compliments his admirer Harriet Mary Capes by saying that "the reader collaborates with the author" (*CL* 2:394) to give meaning to the text. In another letter to Cunninghame Graham, he states that "one writes only half the book; the other half is with the reader" (*CL* 1:370). Accordingly, the eye by which I see Conrad is the same eye by which he and his works see me. In other words, my construction of Conrad's image, based on his *corpus*, is a product of my individual past,[2] and at the same time such a constructed image reveals the capacity of Conrad's art to inspire a particular Chinese reader. This reading process enriches the reader's inner life on one hand and contributes to the interpretation of Conrad on the other, which might add to Conrad studies a Chinese, or more specifically, Confucian perspective.

Since the 1990s, Conrad has become one of the most read and studied Western authors in China.[3] Translations, monographs, graduate theses, and critical essays have sprung up in large numbers, which makes one ponder: Why are Conrad's works so enduring and far-reaching for Chinese readers? Coincidentally, a basic Confucian concept, *Cheng* (诚, sincerity[4]), seems to offer a ready key to this question. According to *The Doctrine of the Mean* (中庸, one of *The Four Books*), "entire sincerity is ceaseless,"[5] meaning if a person possesses absolute sincerity, his influence will be long lasting and far reaching. This essay demonstrates that sincerity is one of Conrad's essential personal traits, which serves as a guiding principle in his treatment of human relationships and his aesthetic handling of art. In the Chinese critical tradition, there is a conviction that "the style is the person" (文如其人). As history shows, there are instances violating this belief: people of vile character produce fine pieces of art. However, the essential tenet that one's temperament permeates and manifests in one's literary creation plays a central role in Chinese literary criticism.[6] In this essay, I will adhere to this long Chinese tradition and argue that the essential personal trait of Conrad, his sincerity, infuses both his life and his works.

Before embarking on a full exposition of Conrad's sincerity, however, attention should be given to his complexity. Conrad declares that his "thought is always multiple" (*CL* 3:492). The meaning of "sincerity" used in his novels and short stories is subtle and nuanced, capturing a full spectrum of the word's implications. For instance, it sometimes indicates purity of emotions, such as when Charles Gould first meets his future wife, and his treatment of her "is the true method of sincerity" (Conrad, *Nostromo* 46). This purity might be tinged with a dark hue, as when Marlow in *Heart of Darkness* calls Kurtz's last words "his final burst of sincerity" (66), and in *The Rover* the abbe says to Arlette, "you must look with fearless sincerity into the darkness of your soul" (352). Sincerity is collocated, from time to time, with inclinations that are negative, as Marlow describes a stranger's way of speaking in "Youth" "with a sincerity in his fury that almost convinced me I had [. . .] sinned against the harmony of the universe" (*Short Stories* 95). Marlow in *Lord Jim* employs sincerity in a similar way: "I was made to look at the convention that lurks in all truth and on the essential sincerity of falsehood" (57). It seems that Conrad treats sincerity neutrally: people can be sincerely good or bad; it signifies only the purity and intensity of feelings and motives. It is not the word, but the person who uses it, just as "ships are all right; it's the men in 'em" (*Mirror* 128). However, if some characters in Conrad's fiction misapply this freedom to choose and violate the untaintedness of sincerity, Conrad the person sticks to sincerity persistently. It is Conrad's sincerity, not his characters', that the present essay aims to tackle. Accordingly, Conrad's non-fiction writings, such as his letters and essays, will be counted on as major sources. With the caveat referred to in footnote 4, this essay also draws upon the Confucian idea, *Cheng*, to illuminate Conrad's sincerity.

The modern Chinese character (*Cheng*, sincerity) is derived from a pictographic word, as the following image shows:

[7]

The Chinese character above consists of two parts. The left part imitates the shape of a tongue, reading *yan* (言), meaning "word"; the right part indicates the look of an ax, reading *Cheng* (成), meaning "to accomplish"; the combination of the two means "to accomplish with words." Why does *Cheng* imply the accomplishment of things through words? The reason lies in its origin. The character 诚 (*Cheng*) is of a left-right structure, with the left part, 言 (*yan*), weighing over the right part, 成 (*Cheng*), in meaning. The character 言 (*yan*, word) was coined in King Wuyi's (武乙) reign in the twelfth century BC and was used solely by the king when offering sacrifices to deities, referring to the words he spoke in prayer. Belief in spirits prevailed in the Shang Dynasty (c. 1600–1046 BC), and people believed that divine blessings could only be won through absolute sincerity; impurity in intention and emotion would induce misfortune. Consequently, *Cheng* in the beginning of its usage signified religious piety—purity of thought and singleness of purpose would make prayers true.[8]

The meaning of *Cheng* evolved through the Shang and Zhou dynasties (1046–256 BC). When it was systematically expounded in *The Doctrine of the Mean*,[9] *Cheng* became a Confucian concept, loaded with ontological and ethical significance. In Chinese philosophy, starting from the *I Ching*,[10] Heaven is considered the entity behind myriad things, "Heaven and earth attract each other and thus all creatures come into being"[11] (Wilhelm 123). Heaven is the creator of man[12] and endows him with nature, namely, his essence of being, "[w]hat Heaven conferred is called the nature" (*Doctrine* 254). As a result, Heaven is "both transcendent and immanent" (Mou 20), and man is inherently united with Heaven through nature.[13] Moreover, the defining quality of Heaven is *Cheng*: "[t]he way of Heaven and Earth may be completely declared in one sentence.—They are *without any doubleness*, and so they produce things in a manner that is unfathomable" (Zisi 291; my emphasis). In Confucian thinking, *Cheng* means "without any doubleness," and it is due to *Cheng* that Heaven and Earth are all embracing and everlasting. This essential quality of Heaven is also imparted to man, whose life mission is to actualize it; "[s]incerity is the way of Heaven. The attainment of sincerity is the way of men" (284).

In chapters 20 through 26 of *The Doctrine of the Mean*, the idea of *Cheng* is elaborated. What is it like to have *Cheng*? How to achieve *Cheng*? And what are the effects of *Cheng*? A saint[14] is the person who manifests *Cheng* completely, realizing fully what is inherently in him, "[w]ithout an effort, [he] hits what is right, and apprehends, without the exercise of thought; [. . .] [he] naturally and easily embodies the right way" (284). However, the ordinary person needs to choose "what is good, and firmly holds it fast" (Zisi 284), so as to obtain *Cheng*. Through strenuous moral effort he may grasp what is good[15] and through laborious work he might procure *Cheng*.[16] Nevertheless, "the achievement being made, it comes to the same thing" (278). That is, after possessing *Cheng* both the saint and the ordinary man will experience similar effects: 1. Self-fulfillment and the fulfillment of others;[17] 2. Proper practice of the Mean;[18] 3. Prophetic vision;[19] 4. To be ceaseless.[20]

It can be concluded that *Cheng*, as a Confucian concept, means purity of thought and singleness of purpose. It is the defining quality of Heaven, the creator of myriad things, and also imparted to man, endowing him with the meaning of being. Man's life-long mission is to cultivate *Cheng* so as to achieve self-realization and complete union with Heaven. However, "Chinese philosophy centers on life" (Mou 6). Instead of laying "the divine as the ultimate basis [of human existence] [. . .] the common human experience is the center upon which the moral order depends" (Tu 86). This Confucian emphasis on "the common human experience" instead of transcendent meaning resonates strongly with Conrad's ethical position:

> The rest is our affair—the laughter, the tears, the tenderness, the indignation, the high tranquility of a steeled heart, the detached curiosity of a

subtle mind—that's our affair! And the unwearied self-forgetful attention to every phase of the living universe reflected in our consciousness may be our appointed task on this earth. (*Mirror* 272)

It can be seen that Conrad suspects "the ethical view of the universe" and proposes that human existence has "a moral end in themselves" (*Mirror* 272). As John Peters puts it, "Conrad concentrated on human relationships, trying to identify a means by which one could construct at least an ephemeral meaning for existence in a universe that Conrad had long since considered to be devoid of any transcendent meaning" ("Literary Response" 35). Therefore, this essay will leave out the transcendent meaning of *Cheng* and use its ethical implications to construct Joseph Conrad's sincerity.

Before continuing, however, it is necessary to remove certain obstacles in the field of Conrad studies. According to Confucianism, *Cheng* is transparent, evident, and bright: "[f]rom being apparent, it becomes manifest. From being manifest, it becomes brilliant" (Zisi 288). In contrast, "obscurity" is considered a key feature of Conrad's character and his literary creation (Watt 2), a term that Ian Watt borrows from E. M. Forster, who famously asks whether "the secret casket of [Conrad's] genius" does not contain "a vapor rather than a jewel" (Forster 346), which reminds us of the equally well-known image related to Marlow and his yarns: "to him the meaning of an episode was not inside like a kernel but outside, enveloping the tale which brought it out only as a glow brings out a haze" (*Heart* 5). The "vapor" and the "haze" prompt the question: Is it possible to find crystal-clear sincerity with such a misty atmosphere of vagueness and uncertainty hanging over Conrad's temperament and his works?

Forster argues further that the vapor might be a result of "the central chasm of [Conrad's] tremendous genius" or the "constant discrepancies between his nearer and further vision" (345). Watt expounds these ideas in more detail: Conrad's "further vision" was very similar to that of his great contemporaries, while his "nearer vision," or his actual range of experience, was not, which engenders his "central chasm" (2). Cutting into this "central chasm," Watt puts forward two confrontational terms, "alienation" and "commitment." Watt thinks Conrad's alienation, "his sense of inward estrangements" (6), is a result of "the characteristic despair of the late Victorian world-view" (3), and his commitment, "a binding engagement of oneself to a course of action which transcends any purely personal advantage," comes from his "years at sea" (7). The two are "in perpetual opposition" (7). Watt argues further that the way out of this dilemma is "to accept the position that fidelity must govern the individual's relation to the outside world, while his inner self must be controlled by restraint and honour" (14). Watt's analysis of Conrad's obscurity is powerful and convincing. However, he polarizes self and society, "the inner and the outer," seemingly unable to bridge these opposing forces so as to view them as the two sides of the same problem. He has given an explanation of the obscurity imposed on Conrad by critics; however, he has not removed it.

When we question Conrad's obscurity, we seldom reflect upon our own "departmental" (Galsworthy 208) or partial mentality. E. M. Forster sees in Conrad "a vapor," John Galsworthy sees in him "the cosmic spirit" (209), Ford Madox Ford sees in him "the point of honor" (Sherry 243), Virginia Woolf sees in him the beauty of Helen (310), and Chinua Achebe sees in him a racist. The many facets disparate readers see testify to Conrad's greatness as an author. More often than not, what we see in Conrad are but reflections of our own selves, and those things we are unable to see with clarity we tend to call "vapor[s]." It is my argument that there is no "central chasm" or "unresolved conflict" (Watt 2) in Conrad, but rather he confronts the problems of his age with undaunted daring and offers it a remedy that we can trace to his experience of the sea. With a clear vision of what the universe is like and man's position within it, Conrad presents both human alienation and human commitment. If alienation is the stern reality, commitment presents a possible solution.

What I am trying to say is that our view of Conrad's obscurity might betray our own inability to see, in spite of his ultimate purpose to "make [us] *see*" (*"Narcissus"* 147). Morever, scholars tend to give a polarized reading of Conrad's alienation and commitment, but for me this shows Conrad's insight into the predicaments of his age and his offering of a solution. Underneath his skepticism, irony, and pessimistic vision, there is his unswerving sincerity as an author—to present life as it is. As he declares, his writings are produced in "perfect single mindedness" (*CL* 1:293) and "in a spirit of piety" (4:113).

However, there is yet another obstacle to eliminate before constructing Conrad's sincerity. It is the query about his "duplicity" as a friend. In Edward Garnett's words, "what a variety of appealing tones Conrad had" (Garnett 20). Doubts about Conrad's sincerity hover in Conrad studies. As the current secretary of the United Kingdom Joseph Conrad Society, Hugh Epstein, wrote to me recently:

> And this is true of his letters: his voice is different to Cunninghame Graham than to Edward Garnett, and different again to his greatest friend, John Galsworthy. Which is the sincere Conrad voice? If it is possible to adopt different voices, and write profound things in each of them, what happens to the notion of "sincerity?" Doesn't sincerity imply integrity, and doesn't integrity point to a unitary, undivided state of mind and being, issuing in a single authentic voice?

Epstein's questionings seem hard to refute. Interestingly, Conrad has an answer for them:

> You would talk differently to a coal-heaver and to a professor. But is this duplicity? I deny it. The truth consists in the genuineness of the feeling, in the genuine recognition of the two men, so similar and so different, as your two partners in the hazard of life. (*Mirror* 58)

What Conrad basically says is that to know people and treat them as they deserve is not duplicity; on the contrary, the genuineness of feeling manifests sincerity. Coincidentally, Conrad's understanding of interpersonal communication corresponds to the Confucian definition of justice (*yi*, 义), "to treat people as they deserve."[21] The truth is, to really know people and treat them accordingly is not for everyone; the mean is for those who know. When a disciple asked Confucius about wisdom, the Master answered, "[k]now your fellow men" (*Analects* 116). Aristotle holds similar ideas:

> it is no easy task to be good. For in everything it is no easy task to find the middle [. . .] to do this to the right person, to the right extent, at the right time, with the right motive, and in the right way, that is not for everyone, nor is it easy; wherefore goodness is both rare and laudable and noble. (*Ethics* 45)

Aristotle thinks that to really know people and treat them in proper ways is virtue. Since it is hard to accomplish, it is rare and noble, deserving of praise. Conrad, as known among his friends, has "a profound sense of the inwardness of things" (Curle 3). In addition, his thought is "constantly for others" (5). If we return to Hugh Epstein's questioning about the various voices employed in Conrad's letters, we will find that Conrad mainly talks about social issues with Cunninghame Graham and Bertrand Russell, about writing with Edward Garnett, about writing and domestic delicacies with John Galsworthy, about moral issues with the Sandersons, with Richard Curle about many things, and with Pinker, mainly business.[22] It is obvious that Conrad writes according to the aptitude and disposition of the addressee,[23] either answering their questions or stating his own opinions. In such sincere and soul-to-soul communications, life-nourishing and sustaining relationships are established. Richard Curle offers a strong testimony to Conrad's sincerity as a friend:

> His friendship was whole-hearted. It was not given freely or widely in the fullest sense, but for those to whom it was so given he would have done

anything. Such was his nature, *such was the simple basis of his complex character.*

His loyalty was touching in its indulgent completeness. He could not bear to see his friends unhappy: in any sorrow or difficulty he would support them, in any outside quarrel they were always right. What they had set their hearts on he tried to bring about [. . .]. (Curle 11; my emphasis)

When so many critics have been occupied with Conrad's obscurity and complexity, Richard Curle is able to seize *the simple basis* of the author's life. In Curle's opinion, Conrad treats friends with entire sincerity, without a single trace of reserve. He would do anything for friends in need. He would help them fulfill their hearts' desire. More importantly for me, Curle's statement above voices the fundamental argument of this essay: underneath the complexity of Conrad's character and literary creation, there is a "simple basis" of his life—sincerity. When we talk about Conrad's sincerity, we are not talking about his perfection. Living under "the unyielding tyranny of circumstances" (*CL* 4:103) as "a needy man" (2:383) and "a tormented spirit" (4:309) in miserable health, Conrad let groans of pain and pleas for pity permeate his letters. However, this essay aims to get through the veil of details at "the simple basis" of his being to see how it shines forth in his life and works.

Reading Conrad side by side with Confucian classics, the deep accord between the two makes one wonder: Has Conrad indeed an "Oriental temperament" (Sherry 250)? One manifestation of Confucian sincerity (*Cheng*, 诚) is to do what is proper to fellow beings, to help them fulfill their selves. As an author of some standing, Conrad nurtured the growth of Ford Madox Ford, John Galsworthy, Hugh Clifford, Richard Curle, and even Garnett, although he is called "literary father" (Garnett 60) by Conrad. The following quotations from *The Doctrine of the Mean* echo Conrad's treatment of his friends:

It is only he who is possessed of the most complete sincerity who can give its full development to his nature. Able to give its full development to his own nature, he can do the same to the nature of other men. (286–87; Legge's translation with my modifications)

To fulfill oneself is the accomplishment of virtue; to fulfill others is the manifestation of wisdom. [. . . .] Whenever entire sincerity is employed, what is done is right. (289–90)

It might be argued that Conrad's capacity to fulfill friends and foster friendships is a strong manifestation of his utter sincerity. Moreover, according to Confucianism, the cultivation of sincerity is a life-long process, a process of becoming. Only saints have full possession of it. As ordinary individuals, we choose "what is good, and firmly [hold] it fast" (284) to move constantly forward along the path of goodness. That is how Conrad functions in his life: "I wish [...] I were more worthy [...] all my life I have tried! tried! tried!" (*CL* 5:10–11) This firmness in longing for what is good and the constant practice of it corroborate the defining attribute of the Confucian *Cheng*.

This essay has tried to cope with two doubts hanging over Conrad's sincerity as an author and as a friend—his obscurity and his duplicity. In removing these hindering forces from the construction of Conrad's sincerity, I have also partly demonstrated Conrad's sincerity as an author—his single-mindedness in presenting life as it is, and his sincerity as a friend—his treatment of friends as they deserve and to help fulfill themselves. Next, I aim to expose deeper affinities between Conrad's sincerity and the Confucian *Cheng* to see how they tackle the following questions: How is sincerity defined? What is the role of sincerity in the universe? And how important is sincerity for human relationships?

A few of Conrad's writings, such as *The Collected Letters*, *The Mirror of the Sea*, and the "Preface to *The Nigger of the "Narcissus*,"[24] offer simple and clear definitions of sincerity:

> Without any mental reservations and in perfect sincerity [...]. (*CL* 2:385)[25]
> I write in perfect sincerity and with no second thoughts at the back of my head [...]. (9:253)
> [...] this book written in perfect sincerity holds back nothing [...]. (*Mirror* 9)

The similarity of these three quotations is striking, indicating Conrad's consistency in the understanding of sincerity over the years.[26] The shared modifier "perfect" shows Conrad's wish to express the purity and intensity of his emotions and intentions. However, this modifier of the highest degree fails, according to the inner urge of Conrad, to articulate fully the unquestionable quality of his sincerity; it is assisted by prepositional or verb phrases to lay bare his internal motivations to his readers. For Conrad, sincerity is "without any mental reservations," "hold[ing] back nothing," and "with no second thoughts." Such expressions correspond to the Confucian definition of *Cheng*, "without doubleness" (Zisi 291).

More importantly, Conrad thinks, sincerity is of primal import within the universe: "[L]ike all fine arts, [the art of handling ships] must be based upon a broad, solid sincerity, which, like a law of nature, rules an infinity of different phenomena" (*Mirror* 58). Conrad's elucidation of sincerity goes beyond the personal level and reaches universal significance. He regards sincerity a fundamental law of nature, ruling myriad phenomena. But how? Zisi (子思, 483–02 BC), the author of *The Doctrine of the Mean*, illuminates this issue: "Sincerity is the end and beginning of things; without sincerity, there would be nothing" (289).

For Conrad, then, all arts have their basis in sincerity; sincerity is the law ruling nature. *The Doctrine of the Mean* attests that sincerity gives birth to all things; without it, nothing. They both seem to stress that creators, whether the creator of myriad things or of fine arts, obey the law of sincerity. Creation is like a mother in her delivery—she is naturally trying her utmost without doubleness of mind or the holding back of effort. It seems, for both Conrad and Confucius, sincerity has its full manifestations in giving birth—it is the primordial force behind the creation of all things, including art.

Then what role does sincerity play in human society? Conrad claims, "it is everything!" (*"Narcissus"* 147):

> In a single-minded attempt of that kind, if one be deserving and fortunate, one may perchance attain to such clearness of sincerity that at last the presented vision of regret or pity, of terror or mirth, shall awaken in the hearts of the beholders that feeling of unavoidable solidarity; of the solidarity in mysterious origin, in toil, in joy, in hope, in uncertain fate—which bind men to each other and all mankind to the visible world. (147)

Conrad is saying that the mission of art is "to hold up [. . .] the rescued fragment before all eyes and in the light of a sincere mood" (147) so as to inspire compassion. Through this "feeling together," human solidarity can be brought about. How can an author make his readers feel together with him? By attaining sincerity. "The one who is purely sincere, can move."[27] The quotation above embodies the core of Conrad's philosophy. For him, the significance of human existence is solidarity, and solidarity is achieved through sincerity. For an individual, through the cultivation of sincerity, he is able to generate human bonds, and consequently fulfill the meaning of his being. Sincerity is considered also the basis of human relationships in Confucianism:

> When those in inferior situations do not obtain the confidence of the sovereign, they cannot succeed in governing the people. There is a way to obtain the confidence of the sovereign; if one is not trusted by his friends, he will not get the confidence of his sovereign. There is a way to being trusted by one's friends; if one is not obedient to his parents, he will not be true to friends. There is a way to being obedient to one's parents; if one, on turning

his thoughts in upon himself, finds a want of sincerity, he will not be obedient to his parents. (Zisi 283–84)

According to Confucianism, the guiding principle of a person's life[28] is to cultivate the self, to manage the household, to govern the state and to rule the country.[29] Only with full self-cultivation can a person be accepted and followed by his household and his people, while the key of self-cultivation is sincerity. It can be seen that both Conrad and Confucius consider sincerity as the cornerstone of human solidarity. However, Conrad's position is more ethical, while the Confucian stance is more politically-based, therefore, the starting point of the two philosophies differs as well. For Conrad, located within "a universe with no transcendental meaning" (Peters, "Voice" 9), the worthiness of human existence is to construct human solidarity through sincerity. On the other hand, Confucianism considers "Heaven and Earth" the benevolent creator, who endows man with his essential nature, *Cheng*, and the significance of human existence is to achieve union with Heaven and Earth through cultivating *Cheng*. Apparently, Conrad and Confucius hold distinct views in regard of the universe. All the same, both of them rest on sincerity as the basis of their life philosophies.

In conclusion, sincerity has not aroused sufficient attention in Conrad studies,[30] maybe because sincerity has not acquired the same pivotal preeminence in Western culture as it has in Confucianism. With the Confucian idea of *Cheng*, the fundamental importance of sincerity within Conrad's philosophy is mirrored forth. Sincerity, for Conrad, means singleness of mind or without mental reservation. It is the foundation of artistic endeavor and it forms the basis of human solidarity, through which one achieves the meaning of being.

ACKNOWLEDGMENTS

My gratitude goes, first of all, to Hugh Epstein and Jeremy Hawthorn, who nurtured the growth of this essay from the very beginning. I am infinitely grateful to Keith Carabine and Linda Dryden, who read the first draft, corrected my errors, and gave minute and invaluable suggestions. Robert Hampson and John Peters were most kind in sharing with me their resources and advising me wisely. The two reviewers for *Conradiana*, Shen Dan and Wang Ning assisted the improvement of the essay. Xu Yong and Yuan Guangtao helped me to find related books and articles.

This research is supported by Li Ka Shing Foundation and Guangdong Planning Office of Philosophy and Social Science: "Joseph Conrad: Chinese Perspectives" (Project No. GD16XWW01).

NOTES

1. I was born in 1977 near Mount Tai, about one hour's drive from Confucius's birthplace Qufu, which was the capital of the Lu State in the Spring and Autumn Period (770–476 BC). I was brought up in an intensely Confucian atmosphere, where people still stuck to Confucian doctrines, such as "be patriotic and loyal to your leaders" (耕忠君爱国), "be affectionate fathers and dutiful sons" (父慈子孝), "farming and learning give a house long prosperity" (读持家远), "a good scholar will make a good official" (学而优则仕), etc. It is amazing that Confucian influences persisted then, after about one hundred years' political and cultural movements and wars, most of which aimed, in one way or another, to diminish Confucian creeds and practices, especially the Great Cultural Revolution. However, I did not realize the most powerful Confucian influence upon a Chinese individual until doing my doctoral studies from 2006 to 2009, under the supervision of an ethical critic, David Heywood Parker (1943–2015). Confucianism is essentially a moral philosophy, which focuses on questions such as, "How should human beings live?" or "What is it good to be?" Its classics, referring mainly to *The Four Books* and *Five Classics* (四书五经), offer its adherents a treasure house of ethical perspectives.

2. In "Joseph Conrad and the Epistemology of Space," John Peters persuasively argues that "one's public and private pasts lead to a distinct" view of space (100). Here I will similarly argue that a reader's public and private pasts lead to his or her distinct interpretation of a literary text.

3. Cf. An Ning, "Conrad Studies in Mainland China, 1924–2014."

4. "Sincerity" is the most widely accepted English translation for the Confucian *Cheng*. However, unlike *Cheng*, sincerity does not have ontological connotations. The present essay adopts this conventional translation, with the awareness that sincerity is not an equivalent of *Cheng*. According to Robert Allyn, "sincerity" is from Latin, meaning "without wax" (183). It later means, "in a man, that his good qualities, whatever they may be, are pure and unalloyed, sweet, and precisely what they are held out to be" (183). According to Patricia M. Ball, before the nineteenth century "sincerity [. . .] was used to affirm purity of belief, genuine doctrine, freedom from theological duplicity," and in the nineteenth century it was used as "an artistic criterion" (1). It can be seen that "sincerity" as an English word signifies the genuineness of things, the pure quality or loyal attitude of human beings, or artistic virtues, without transcendental implications.

5. "至诚无息". From chapter 26 of *The Doctrine of the Mean*. Translation mine. Unlike the other three of *The Four Books*, namely, *The Analects*, *Mencius*, and *The Great Learning*, which have more than one or even a great variety of English translations, *The Doctrine of the Mean* has only one widely accepted 1893 English translation by James Legge, which the present essay relies on, with occasional exceptions.

6. Cf. Jiang Yin, "Wenru Qiren—Yige Gudian Mingti de Heli Neihan yu Shiyong Xiandu" ["The Style Being the Man?—The Reasonable Connotation and Scope of Application of a Classical Proposition"] 文如其人?—一个古典命题的合理内涵与适用限度. *Seeking Truth.* vol. 28, no. 6, 2001, pp. 82–9.

7. This image is *Zhuanshu* (篆书, seal character), which maintains the features of the pictographic character, an earlier form of writing.

8. Cf. Wu Fanming, et al., "An Analysis of Sincerity in *The Doctrine of the Mean.*"

9. According to the *Record of the Grand Historian* (史记), *The Doctrine of the Mean* was composed by Confucius's grandson, Zisi (子思, 483–402 BC). In the Han Dynasty (206 BC–220 AD), this treatise was collected into *The Book of Rites* (礼记). Later, Zhu Xi (朱熹, 1130–1200 AD) of the Song Dynasty (960–1279 AD) combined it with *The Analects, Mencius*, and *The Great Learning* into *The Four Books*.

10. The *I Ching* is generally recognized as the beginning of Chinese philosophy: "[N]early all that is greatest and most significant in the three thousand years of Chinese cultural history has either taken its inspiration from this book, or has exerted an influence on the interpretation of its text" (Wilhelm xlvii).

11. "天地感而万物化生". Moreover, in *I Ching*, heaven is considered the creative force or "the primal power" (Wilhelm 3) while earth is "the receptive" (10).

12. "Man" is used here, by following the Confucian tradition, to stand for the human species, without sexual prejudices, on my part. *The Four Books* quotes heavily from *The Book of Songs* to prove its ideas. In *The Book of Songs* (诗经), a line says, "[h]eaven produces people, guiding them with principles" (天生烝民, 有物有则) (895; my translation).

13. This idea of heaven-endowed nature resembles the creation of man in the Bible and Greek mythology. In the Hebrew and Greek traditions, the divine breathed into the nostrils of man and he received his spirit. Consequently, man is bound to the divine through his spirit. In Chinese culture, man is united with his creator, Heaven, through his nature. According to Karl Jaspers, in the Axial Period were born "the fundamental categories within which we still think today" (Jaspers 2), which might explain this deep accord in regard to creation among ancient Greek, Hebrew, and Chinese civilizations. However, the origin of man is different according to Buddhism, another religion Jaspers discusses. In Buddhism, although it is believed that "all living beings have the Buddha spirit" (*Nirvana Sutra* 103), Buddha is not the creator. All things, including human beings, come from "a combination of four primary elements, which are earth, water, fire, and wind" (*Surangama Sutra* 531). In that case, the Buddha spirit is not endowed by a creator; instead, it refers to "every person's potential to become a Buddha" (Zhao 2), which means all living beings have the capacity to perceive the empty nature of things, so as to avoid desire and suffering and finally achieve the ultimate wisdom and Nirvana. Buddhism spread to China during the Han Dynasty (202 BC–220 AD). When its classics were first translated in Eastern Han (25–220 AD), Confucian terms were used to make translations lucid. At the same time, Confucianism assimilated Buddhism in its own development. In the Song Dynasty (960–1279 AD), the fusion of the two, including Taosim, reached its zenith; scholars then proposed "Three Religions in One (三教合一)" (Hong, *passim*). It might be argued that the influence of Buddhism in Confucianism is undeniable even if it should be relegated to the background, to the subconscious, as it were. The present essay adopts the Confucian idea of *Cheng* without consciously probing into its Buddhist connotations.

14. It has been understood throughout Chinese history that saints do not live among us, because when a person claims to be a saint, his immodesty makes him less than a saint. Saints are usually named so by people after their death. As virtuous as Confucius was, he often scrutinized his own deficiencies instead of thinking himself as a saint. For instance, "[i]n the way of the superior man there are four things, to not one of which have I as yet attained" (Zisi 265); "I am not one who was born in the possession of knowledge; I am one who is fond of antiquity, and earnest in seeking it there" (*Analects* 67).

15. "To this attainment there are requisite the extensive study of what is good, accurate inquiry about it, careful reflection on it, the clear discrimination of it, and the earnest practice of it" (Zisi 285).

16. "If another man succeed by one effort, he will use a hundred efforts. If another man succeed by ten efforts, he will use a thousand" (Zisi 285).

17. A person of *Cheng* can fully realize his nature and help to fulfill the nature of other people and things: "[i]t is only he who is possessed of the most complete sincerity that can exist under heaven, who can transform" (Zisi 288).

18. A person of *Cheng* is able to do what is appropriate always: "[t]he superior man [. . .] always maintains the Mean" (Zisi 257).

19. A person of *Cheng* is a person of insight and knowledge. He can perceive what is hidden to distracted eyes: "[w]hen calamity or happiness is about to come, the good shall certainly be foreknown by him, and the evil also. Therefore the individual possessed of the most complete sincerity is like a spirit" (Zisi 288).

20. A person of *Cheng* would form a trinity with Heaven and Earth: "he can assist the transforming and nourishing powers of Heaven and Earth" (Zisi 287). His influence will last long and reach far: "to entire sincerity there belongs ceaselessness" (290).

21. "义者, 宜也." From chapter 20 of *The Doctrine of the Mean*, my translation. Legge translates this as: "Righteousness is the accordance of actions with what is right" (Zisi 276).

22. When translating *The Selected Letters of Joseph Conrad* in 2019, Laurence Davies kindly allowed me to make new arrangements of the letters. I grouped letters to the same addressee together and then arranged the addressees according to the time they first knew Conrad. In this way, the topics talked about to each addressee became prominent.

23. As one of the reviewers suggests, the Buddha, just as Conrad, uses expedient means, chosen "according to the aptitude and disposition of the addressee" in order to communicate his sincerity, his truth. The Buddha explains in *The Lotus Sutra*, "I know that living beings have various desires. Attachments that are deeply implanted in their minds. Taking cognizance of this basic nature of theirs, I will therefore use various causes and conditions, words of simile and parable, and the power of expedient means and expound the Law for them" (*Lotus* 39). Buddha's way of teaching resonates strongly with Confucius's idea of "Teaching according to Aptitude (因材施教)," as the master explains to his disciples: "Ch'iu holds himself back. It is for this reason that I tried to urge him on. Yu has the energy of two men. It is for this reason that I tried to hold him back" (*Analects* 109).

24. Sincerity is used eighty-four times in *The Collected Letters*, four times in *The Mirror*, and once in the Preface to *The Nigger of the "Narcissus."*

25. It is known that the Conrad-Pinker relationship is rather tricky. This quote is from a letter to Pinker at the beginning of their author-agent relationship, which has not gone through trials yet. Here, Conrad hands over his affairs to Pinker with outspoken trust and sincerity. In the following twenty years, their mutual understanding and support survived numerous crises and matured finally into real friendship. When Pinker died in 1922, Conrad admitted: "P's death has been a real blow" (*CL* 7:417) and their bond was "as strong as the nearest relationship" (7:416).

26. Quote 1 is from a letter to Pinker in 1902; the date and addressee of quote 2 are unidentified, but according to the editors it is probably written between 1917 and 1924;

quote 3 must be written no earlier than 1917, since starting from that year, Conrad began Author's Notes for the collected edition of his works.

27. "唯天下至诚, 为能化". From chapter 23 of *The Doctrine of the Mean*, my translation.

28. The target readers of *The Four Books* are those who can receive education and play a role in the management of the country.

29. 修齐治平.

30. There is one article available about sincerity in Conrad, that by Ella Ophir, "Sincerity and Self-Revelation in Joseph Conrad," which focuses more on the unattainability of sincerity in Conrad's major works instead of discussing Conrad's own sincerity. I also consulted John Peters, who wrote *Joseph Conrad's Critical Reception* and has been keeping records of new publications in Conrad studies, about the study of Conrad's sincerity. He kindly answered that Ella Ophir's essay was the only one he knew of that focused on the study of sincerity in Conrad.

WORKS CITED

Achebe, Chinua. "An Image of Africa: Racism in Conrad's *Heart of Darkness*." *Heart of Darkness*, edited by Paul B. Armstrong, W.W. Norton, 1991, pp. 336–49.

Allyn, Robert. "Sincerity." *The R. I. Schoolmaster*, vol. 3, no. 6, 1857, p. 183.

The Analects. Translated by D.C. Lau. Penguin Books, 1979.

Aristotle. *The Nicomachean Ethics*. Translated by David Ross, Oxford University Press, 1980.

Ball, Patricia M. "Sincerity: The Rise and Fall of a Critical Term." *Modern Language Review*, vol. 59, no. 1, 1964, pp. 1–11.

Barthes, Roland. *The Pleasure of the Text*. Translated by Richard Miller, Hill and Wang, 1998.

Cheng, Junying, and Jiang Jianyuan, eds. *The Book of Songs: An Annotated Edition*. China Publishing House, 2016.

Conrad, Joseph. *The Collected Letters of Joseph Conrad*. Edited by Laurence Davies, et al., 9 vols., Cambridge University Press, 1983–2008.

———. *Heart of Darkness*. Edited by Paul B. Armstrong, W. W. Norton, 1991.

———. *Lord Jim*. Edited by Thomas C. Moser, W. W. Norton, 1968.

———. *The Mirror of the Sea and A Personal Record*. Edited by Keith Carabine, Wordsworth Editions, 2008.

———. *The Nigger of the "Narcissus."* Edited by Robert Kimbrough, W. W. Norton, 1979.

———. *Nostromo*. Edited by Jacques Berthoud and Mara Kalnins, Oxford University Press, 2007.

———. *Selected Short Stories* and *The Rover*. Edited by Keith Carabine, Wordsworth Editions, 2011.

Curle, Richard. "The Last of Conrad." The Joseph Conrad Society (UK), n.d.

Epstein, Hugh. Correspondent, email message to author, Feb. 21, 2020.

Forster, E. M. "Joseph Conrad: A Note." *Conrad: The Critical Heritage*, edited by Norman Sherry, Routledge and Kegan Paul, 1973, pp. 345–48.

Galsworthy, John. "Joseph Conrad: A Disquisition." *Conrad: The Critical Heritage*, edited by Norman Sherry, Routledge and Kegan Paul, 1973, pp. 203–9.

Garnett, Edward. *Letters from Joseph Conrad 1895–1924*. The Bobbs-Merrill Company, 1928.
Hong, Xiuping. "Relations among Confucianism, Buddhism and Taoism and the Development of Chinese Buddhism." *Journal of Nanjing University*, 2002, vol. 3, pp. 81–93.
Jaspers, Karl. *The Origin and Goal of History*. Translated by Michael Bullock, Routledge, 2010.
Jiang, Yin. "The Style Being the Man? The Reasonable Connotation and Scope of Application of a Classical Proposition." *Seeking Truth*, vol. 28, no. 6, 2001, pp. 82–89.
The Lotus Sutra. Translated by Burton Watson, Columbia University Press, 1993.
Mou, Zongsan. *Zhongguo Zhexue de Benzhi* [*The Essence of Chinese Philosophy*] 中国哲学的本质. Shanghai, Shanghai Classics Publishing House, 2007.
Ning, An. "Conrad Studies in Mainland China, 1924–2014." *The Conradian*, vol. 41, no. 1, 2016, pp. 87–101.
The Nirvana Sutra. Translated by Mark L. Blum, Bukkyo Dendo Kyokai America, 2013.
Ophir, Ella. "Sincerity and Self-Revelation in Joseph Conrad." *The Modern Language Review*, vol. 107, no. 2, 2012, pp. 341–63.
Peters, John. "'A Voice Crying in the Wilderness': Joseph Conrad's Lasting Legacy." *Yearbook of Conrad Studies (Poland)*, vol. 13, 2018, pp. 7–15.
———. "Joseph Conrad and the Epistemology of Space." *Philosophy and Literature*, vol. 40, no. 1, 2016, pp. 98–123.
———. "Joseph Conrad's Literary Response to the First World War." *College Literature*, vol. 39, no. 4, 2012, pp. 34–45.
Rosenblatt, Louise M. *The Reader, The Text, The Poem: The Transactional Theory of the Literary Work*. Southern Illinois University Press, 1994.
Sherry, Norman, ed. *Conrad: The Critical Heritage*. Routledge and Kegan Paul, 1973.
The Surangama Sutra. Translated by Hsuan Hua, Buddhist Text Translation Society, 2009.
Tu, Weiming. *An Insight of Chung-yung*. People's Publishing House, 2008.
Wilhelm, Richard, trans. *I Ching*. Translated into English by Gary F. Baynes, Penguin Books, 1967.
Watt, Ian. *Essays on Conrad*. Cambridge University Press, 2000.
Woolf, Virginia. *The Common Reader*. Harcourt, Brace and Company, 1925.
Wu, Fanming, et al. "An Analysis of Sincerity in *The Doctrine of the Mean*." *Journal of Hunan University* (Social Science Edition), vol. 14, no. 4, 2000, pp. 16–20.
Zhao, Puchu. *Fojiao Changshi* [*The Essentials of Buddhism*] 佛教常识. Beijing, Beijing Publishing House, 2003.
Zisi. "The Doctrine of the Mean." *The Chinese Classics*. Translated by James Legge, Shanghai, Joint Publishing Company, 2014, pp. 251–305.

Dark Borneo: Yong-Ping Li's Reworkings of *Heart of Darkness* and *Lord Jim* in *The End of the River*

TUNG-AN WEI

NATIONAL YANG MING CHIAO TUNG UNIVERSITY, TAIWAN

Keywords: Borneo, *The End of the River*, *Heart of Darkness*, *Lord Jim*, rewriting

ABSTRACT

Although Joseph Conrad wrote sixteen works set in the Malay Archipelago, there are very few discussions of his reception in Malaysia or Indonesia. To address this critical issue, I examine Malaysian-Taiwanese novelist Yong-Ping Li's two-volume novel, *The End of the River*. I argue that Li repurposes Conrad's *Heart of Darkness* and *Lord Jim* to critique British, European, and Australian men's abuse and desertion of Indigenous women in the years leading up to 1962. Though there is no neat correspondence between Conrad's and Li's plots, Li frames his examination of the "heart of darkness," namely, moral corruption, as an expedition upriver in the rainforest, where white men "go native" and rape Indigenous women. Li additionally repurposes several related phrases, most notably the imperial rhetoric of light penetrating darkness. Li subverts such a rhetoric by detailing how the would-be light—such as Catholic priests and white government officials—sexually exploits the Indigenous women. Moreover, Li's characters share the same impulses to relate personal stories and rumors as do Conrad's. Several characters, like Conrad's Jim, are surrounded by imperial myths. More significantly, by constructing various avid storytellers, Li recuperates the conventionally suppressed voice of Indigenous women. Conrad's tropes, milieu, and characterizations are all instrumental in shedding light on the issue of sexual exploitation in Indonesia in the mid-twentieth century.

Although Joseph Conrad wrote sixteen works set in the Malay Archipelago, there are very few discussions of his reception in Malaysia or Indonesia.[1] To address this critical issue, I examine Malaysian-Taiwanese novelist Yong-Ping Li 李永平's two-volume novel, *The End of the River* (2008, 2010).[2] I argue that Li repurposes Conrad's *Heart of Darkness* (1899) and *Lord Jim* (1900) to critique British, European, and Australian men's abuse and subsequent desertion of Indigenous women. Though there is no neat correspondence between Conrad's and Li's plots, Li frames his examination of the "heart of darkness," namely, white men's moral corruption, as an expedition upriver in the rainforest, where white men "go native" and rape Indigenous women. Li additionally repurposes several related phrases, most notably the imperial rhetoric of light penetrating darkness. Li subverts such a rhetoric by detailing how the would-be light—such as Catholic priests and white government officials—sexually exploits the Indigenous women. Moreover, Li's characters share the same impulses to relate stories and rumors as do Conrad's, through which Li recuperates the conventionally suppressed voice of Indigenous women and develops his trenchant critique of sexual exploitation. Through this first sustained analysis of Li's reworkings of Conrad's tropes, milieu, and characterizations, I not only contribute to Conrad studies but also offer an alternative interpretation of *The End of the River*. Li told Zi-Ping Sun in a 2010 interview that "This novel surpasses politics. I hope that readers look beyond the politics and find the higher meaning of the novel, for example, the things about human nature [. . .]. This is why in the novel I repeatedly mention the novel *Heart of Darkness*" (n.p.). As I will argue, Li's "heart of darkness" is better understood as a specific critique of white men's sexual exploitation of Indigenous women rather than a comment on the universal deterioration of human nature.

Set in West Kalimantan, Indonesia, in 1962, *The End of the River* opens with the protagonist, a fifteen-year-old Chinese settler named Yong, sitting on a ship to Pontianak from Kuching, the Crown Colony of Sarawak. In Pontianak, he meets his father's old friend, the thirty-eight-year-old Dutch expatriate Christina Maria Van Loon, who is the heiress to a rubber plantation on the delta outside of Pontianak and who was a comfort woman (a euphemism for military sex slaves) during the Japanese occupation of Borneo from 1942 to 1945.[3] The story is told by an older Yong to a girl, Zhu Ling, at roughly the same time when the novel was published in the first decade of the twenty-first century. Sitting in his home in Taiwan, Yong recounts his trip up the Kapuas River with Christina to Batu Tiban, the sacred mountain of the Dayaks located on the borders between Sarawak and East Kalimantan. Li stages the trip as a rite of passage and an exotic expedition for a group of thirty white people, mostly from the United Kingdom and its former colonies, who soon succumb to excessive violence, lust, and drinking. It is in this context that the novel situates Yong's sexual initiation and unusual romance with Christina, a romance that culminates in their lovemaking on the top of Batu Tiban.

Given that Li is almost exclusively known to Sinophone studies, let me start with a short introduction to his career and poetics. A second-generation Chinese settler in the Crown Colony of Sarawak, Li spent most of his early years in Chinese-medium schools (and very briefly in English-medium schools) in Kuching before moving to Taiwan to attend college in 1967, majoring in English.[4] He later went to the United States to pursue an M.A. and a Ph.D., both in Comparative Literature. After receiving his Ph.D. from Washington University in St. Louis in 1982, he settled in Taiwan and began teaching in universities intermittently, while also writing and translating at the same time. In 1987, Li became a Taiwanese citizen and renounced his Malaysian citizenship (Sarawak became part of Malaysia in 1963).[5] A highly acclaimed author, Li won the National Award for the Arts in 2015, one of the highest arts honors in Taiwan.

Michaela Bronstein's *Out of Context: The Uses of Modernist Fiction* (2018) offers a useful theoretical framework for outlining Li's repurposing of Conrad. One of Bronstein's central claims is that disenfranchised midcentury writers such as Ngũgĩ wa Thiong'o repurpose the modernist forms of Conrad for new progressive ends. As Bronstein points out, Ngũgĩ's *A Grain of Wheat* (1967) and *Petals of Blood* (1977) do not rewrite Conrad's plots, nor do their meanings depend on allusions (148). But Conrad's achronology, multiple perspectives, and the idea put forth in *Nostromo* (1904) that there is no uninvolved perspective on history are all useful to Ngũgĩ for addressing the moral stakes of involvement in political events and for urging readers to take a stand (113). Influence study, which privileges the agency of the influencer at the expense of the later author, is inadequate because it fails to account for Conrad's particular appeal to Ngũgĩ and his lack of derivativeness. Ngũgĩ tends to view literature in Kenya as free to draw from—or to reject—both European and African traditions (Bronstein 146). Tradition and originality are not conceptualized as opposing terms for Ngũgĩ, contrary to classic theories of influence from Harold Bloom to Christopher Ricks.

Influence study is similarly inadequate to explain Conrad's appeal to Li. Li is deeply rooted in the Chinese literary tradition even as he is also well-versed in Western literature. He draws from both traditions to craft *The End of the River* without any qualms about being unoriginal. Kim-Chew Ng, a prominent critic of Malaysian Sinophone literature, points out that Li's Sinophilia far exceeds that of his contemporaries (including diasporic writers and those born and raised in China) (*Yong-Ping Li Studies* 58). Critics generally agree that Li taps into Chinese literary tradition to forge an "authentically pure" Chinese cultural identity in his earlier works, such as *Retribution: The Jiling Chronicles* and *Haidong Blues: A Fable of Taipei* (Groppe, *Sinophone Malaysian* 77, 188).[6] In a preface that reads like an art manifesto, Li explains that he sought to "rectify the Americanized and the Japanized Chinese in vogue in Taiwan" and "preserve the purity and dignity of the Chinese language [...] through the linguistic style in this book" (*Retribution* i-ii; my translation). The Chinese language continues to occupy a central role in his later works such as *The End of the River* and its prequel, *The Snow Falls in Clouds: Recollections of a Borneo Childhood*, for a different reason. According to Li, he chose to write in Chinese instead of English—he is bilingual since he grew up in a British colony—because the "copious, euphonic, and image-like vocabulary" of the Chinese language "enables [him] to capture the rainforest more vividly" (*River* 1:xv-xvi; my translation).

To investigate how Li reworks Conrad's novels to specifically critique sexual exploitation, I will first discuss Li's intersections with Conrad in terms of poetics and storyworlds. In a 2012 interview with *The Beijing News*, Li explains that he frequently refers to William Somerset Maugham, Rudyard Kipling, and Conrad in his work

> because I grew up reading their Malay fiction and was familiar with their portrayals of the Malay Archipelago. [...] Maugham and Kipling had no influence on me at all because in my mind they were popular writers. Conrad was different; he was a novelist of the high artistic achievement. His views of writing, especially his focus on visuality, gave me immense inspiration. (n.p.; my translation)

Let us first take up Li's comment on the issue of visuality. Li's rainforest is never short of the elements that constitute the iconic landscape of the Conradian jungle: the towering trees, the thick fog, the driving rain, and the flashes of lightning and thunder. Additionally, both Conrad and Li frequently offer an aerial view of the terrain. For instance, the rivers in *Heart of Darkness* and *The End of the River* are consistently described as yellow snakes (Li, *River* 1:119). More significantly, Li repurposes Conrad's motif of cartography in *Heart of Darkness* to visualize the expansive scope of the upriver journey and the spheres of influence of the countries that colonized and otherwise controlled Sarawak and West Kalimantan in the years leading up to 1962. Yong inherits from Marlow a passion for world maps, which is somehow connected to their shared fascination with rivers (1:240). Marlow recalls:

Now when I was a little chap I had a passion for maps. I would look for hours at South America, or Africa or Australia and lose myself in all the glories of exploration. [. . . .] But there was in it one river especially, a mighty big river that you could see on the map, resembling an immense snake uncoiled, with its head in the sea, its body at rest curving afar over a vast country and its tail lost in the depths of the land. And as I looked at the map of it in a shop window it fascinated me like a snake would a bird— a silly little bird. (Conrad, *Youth* 48)

Similarly, Yong tells us that "As a child, as an ethnic Chinese, I liked to collect and read various kinds of maps. While growing up in the Crown Colony of Sarawak, I inevitably saw [. . .] maps that are annotated in English or Dutch and that use the primary colors of red, blue, and white to signify the spheres of influence of various empires" (Li, *River* 2:303). Li's color-coded maps to a certain degree recall the map of the partition of Africa that we see in the Company's offices in *Heart of Darkness*: "There was a vast amount of red—good to see at any time because one knows that some real work is done in there, a deuce of a lot of blue, a little green, smears of orange, and, on the East Coast, a purple patch to show where the jolly pioneers of progress drink the jolly lager-beer" (Conrad, *Youth* 50–51). But for Li, maps are not merely a means of critiquing colonialism and its misrepresentation of the Other as "a blank space" or "a place of darkness" (48). In *The End of the River*, we see a range of worldviews—that of the British, the Japanese, and the Indigenous people— which project different maps.[7] Yong encounters a 1937 Japanese map toward the end of his journey, which, in contrast to all the other maps which Yong grew up reading, positions Japan, China, and the Pacific Ocean in the middle (Li, *River* 2:304). In this map, "Japan is like a golden five-clawed dragon which reigned the north hemisphere supremely" (2:304). Li's novel additionally contains two other cartographic moments, one recording the exact coordinates of present-day Borneo,[8] the other registering the Kenyah tribal leader's personal understanding of the terrain through his peripatetic journey. These map-reading scenes, positioned at the beginning, middle, and end of *The End of the River*, collectively hint at the history of the lands which Yong traverses, namely the Crown Colony of Sarawak and West Kalimantan, the latter of which was occupied by the Japanese during the Second World War and subsequently declared independence from the Netherlands in 1945.

In *Lord Jim* as well as in *The End of the River*, the primitive landscape is associated with sexuality and the female body. In *Lord Jim*, readers are introduced to Patusan in the following description: "At a point on the river about forty miles from the sea, where the first houses come into view, there can be seen rising above the level of the forests the summits of two steep hills very close together and separated by what looks like a deep fissure, the cleavage of some mighty stroke" (167–68). Padmini Mongia, for example, has discussed the 'womb-like enclosure' of Patusan implied by this portrayal ("Ghosts" 7).[9] Similarly, Jim's prospects in Patusan are consistently coded in marital terms, such as in the following example: "his opportunity sat veiled by his side like an Eastern bride waiting to be uncovered by the hand of the master" (*Lord Jim* 184). Li goes further than Conrad to explicitly connect the native land and Indigenous women in terms of (neo)colonial subjugation in lurid detail. In *The End of the River*, the boats that carry the employees of the Japanese logging company are described as "bayonets that aim at the heart of Borneo and penetrate the virgin rainforest" (1:272). As Ng has pointed out, Komatsu bulldozers are a symbol of the modern phallus that violates the Borneo rainforest ("Death" 249). Just as the bulldozers of the neocolonialist Japanese "serial-rape" the land (*River* 1:287), white government officials and Catholic priests, the remnant of Dutch colonialism, rape the Indigenous women, as I will argue.

Li not only strives "to make you *see*," as Conrad aims to do, but he provides abundant sensory details of sound and smell to depict the people inhabiting Borneo (Conrad, *"Narcissus"* 7; original emphasis). For the most part, the Borneo rainforest seems to have a soundscape similar to that of the Congolese jungle, one that contrasts Indigenous people's drum rolls with "primordial silence" (Li, *River* 1:62, 2:273). Marlow writes that "We penetrated deeper and deeper into the heart of darkness. It was very quiet there. At night sometimes the roll of drums behind the curtain of trees would run up the river and remain sustained faintly, as if hovering in the air high over our heads, till the first break of the day" (Conrad, *Youth* 79). Similarly, Yong recalls "the roll of drums—made of human skins—originating from the heart of Borneo, accompanying the sunset on the river" (Li, *River* 2:89). In both texts, drum rolls are screened by the rainforest and metonymically represent the daily activities of the Indigenous people. But Yong does not dwell on the significance of the sound, unlike Marlow, who wonders "whether this meant war, peace, or prayer" (Conrad, *Youth* 79) and speculates that the sound comes "perhaps with as profound a meaning as the sound of bells in a Christian country" (61). Li's prose also transports us to Borneo by recreating the olfactory landscape of the tropics. Yong notices the pungent smell of "primeval" mud (Conrad, *Youth* 69; Li, *River* 1:30). In fact, smell is paramount in *The End of the River* as it virtually becomes an index of identity. The distinctive smell-profiles of Pontianak (the hodgepodge of various ethnic foods) and Christina (her cheese-like odor mixed with soap) metonymically tell us about their respective history, as cheese and soap are always associated with foreign cultures in this novel. As Yong notes, cheese is his least favorite Western food (Li, *River* 1:65), while soap is a signifier of "another culture" (1:264, 2:90).

Li is moreover inspired by Conrad's practices of oral storytelling, including the use of frame narrative, and more importantly the circulation of imperial narratives.[10] David Der-Wei Wang has briefly remarked in his foreword to *The End of the River* that "Sometimes self-mockingly, Li deftly alludes to, on the one hand, the exotic wilderness in the styles of Maugham and Kipling, and, on the other, the self-exploration of the 'heart of darkness' by Joseph Conrad and V.S. Naipaul" (*River* 1:v; my translation). Building on but crucially departing from Wang, I suggest that Yong participates in a lineage of adventurer-storytellers, including Conrad's Marlow, Robert Louis Stevenson's Jim Hawkins and Dr. Livesey, and H. Rider Haggard's Horace Holly, because Yong narrates his experience as a British subject traversing postcolonial Kalimantan and perpetuates many imperial narratives.[11] In addition to Yong's own expedition to Batu Tiban and his exoticizations of the Indigenous people, as I will discuss, the impulses of imperial adventure can be detected in Yong's characterization of Sir Andrew Simpson, a British explorer and founder of a museum in Sarawak specializing in the cultures of the Dayaks. Yong tells us that "unlike Jim, Simpson would never desert the ship because it is a matter of honor" when Simpson travels across the watershed (*River* 2:25). Simpson, who is spotted reading *Lord Jim* on the expedition, is known for his neatness, Englishness, gentlemanly behavior, and sense of honor. Simpson, more thoroughly than Jim, fits the stereotypes of the imperial hero of adventure fiction as described by Linda Dryden and Andrea White. The text reports that Simpson was awarded the Order of the British Empire because of his heroic thousand-mile expedition, in which he single-handedly entered the rainforest from Sarawak, went upriver from British Borneo, climbed over the watershed, entered Dutch Borneo, and finally arrived at the shore of the Celebes Sea (1:70, 74). Yong also mentions that, when he was in his second year in the Chinese-medium junior high school, the school was ordered by the government to teach Borneo native history and culture by using evolutionary theory and, paradoxically, the Christian concept of creation.[12] Simpson is enshrined in this fictional textbook (1:70–71), and throughout the novel he is consistently referred to as a "living legend" (2:287). Yong further models Simpson on a paradigmatic imperial hero, Sir James Brooke, who is one of the prototypes of Tom Lingard and Tuan Jim (Allen 200; White 103).[13] Simpson is "like Conrad's Jim [. . .] and the legendary Rajah James Brooke, who goes deep into the jungle single-handedly, with his guns, bullets, and magic; who builds his dynasty in Sarawak by commanding the Iban head-hunters, the Malay nobles, the Indian mercenaries, and the Chinese miners [...] but who is not blessed with any children" (2:300). But Simpson is crucially distinguished from Brooke because he does not study the Dayaks to rule them.[14] Moreover, it is significant that Yong's rendition of the Brooke myth omits some controversial aspects, especially the massacre of the villages of the "pirates."[15] In turn, the imperial myths which Yong recounts not only suggest that his world is to a certain extent contiguous with Conrad's, but also align Yong with his literary predecessors, Marlow and Jim, who are also deeply immersed in romantic imperial adventures, as countless Conrad scholars have discussed.

The racism entailed by Yong's visually-intense, imperialist-evocative storytelling also harks back to Conrad. Though Li told Zi-Ping Sun in a 2010 interview that his descriptions of Borneo mainly came from his childhood memory, the rainforest is first and foremost a space for exotic spectacle rather than nostalgic reminiscence. Yong's graphic depictions of the Dayak people underscore the Western visitors' sexist and racist impressions of Indigenous cultures.[16] For instance, Yong claims that women's breasts and men's *palang* (ampallang)[17] are the two things that Westerners are most interested in (1:241). Whenever an Iban woman appears, characters gaze at her breasts, which are repeatedly described as "brown papayas" (1:145). What Yong and the Western travelers can imagine and see in the daily life of a Dayak woman is serving dinner, entertaining guests, and bathing in the river. As for the Iban men, the focus is almost exclusively on their *palang* and their tattoos, such as those that indicate how many heads they have hunted. Sometimes Li's rainforest even takes on an eroticized atmosphere, replicating the white characters' lust for Indigenous women. In this respect, Li's novel seems to resemble nineteenth-century travel writing and ethnographic fiction that reproduce lurid descriptions of what they believed to be the most crucial characteristics of the other culture (Griffith 25). If we take Yong's view as the author's, as many critics do, Li ironically perpetuates the racism of the Western writers that he condemns in his 2012 interview in *The Beijing News*.[18] Nevertheless, Yong and Li should not be conflated, not least because Li's somewhat racist poetics is at odds with his critique of white men's exploitation of Indigenous women. In my view, Li employs racial stereotypes not because he necessarily believes in them but because they are useful for his narrative project. That is, Li's account of Indigenous people is comparable to Conrad's complex deployment of African stereotypes in *Heart of Darkness* insofar as both authors' racist poetics are part and parcel of their (post)colonial critique.[19]

So far, I have explored the extent to which Li's poetics and storyworld converge with Conrad's and how Li sets the stage for his social commentary. I will now move on to discuss how Li repurposes the tropes from *Heart of Darkness* to indict white men for abuse of Indigenous women. Drawing upon the trope of "going mad" in the jungle, Li creates a rainforest that seems to have a sinister influence over its visitors. Alison Groppe is correct when she briefly comments that *The End of the River* "recount[s] an uncanny journey into 'the heart of darkness' that transpires physically and emotionally" ("Writer-Wanderer" 909). But Groppe stops short of pinpointing the Victorian genre of imperial gothic, with which both Li and Conrad engage. As Patrick Brantlinger theorizes, the genre centrally concerns a European man who "goes native" in the jungle, succumbs to the lure of dark women, and regresses to primitivism, savagery, and infantilism. Yong notices that white people "go mad" and become less civilized even in the early stage of the journey (Li, *River* 1:106). Indeed, Christina has warned Yong that he "might encounter demons, ghosts, and ghost-like sinister people in the rainforest" before he embarks on the expedition (1:23). Not only do people have tantrums, but they also exhibit violence, lust, and excessive drinking (1:268), including the seduction and rape of Indigenous women by white people in the rainforest. One member of the expedition even contracts syphilis after waking up from a drinking party hosted by a young Dayak man named Nelson Darius Syphilis Bihai, who joins the expedition uninvited (1:266). What exactly happens during that party is never told outright, but Yong wakes up to find everyone, including himself, naked and heaped upon one another like corpses the next morning (1:248). It seems that Yong also "goes native."

In addition to the trope of "going mad" in the jungle, Li also refers to "the heart of darkness" and other related phrases, such as the imperial rhetoric of light penetrating darkness. The Congo and Li's Borneo are both described as "the dark places of the earth" penetrated by colonial powers and Christianity.[20] Yong tells us that the Borneo rainforest is "dark, mysterious, unfathomable. It constantly bewilders the soul of a Chinese youth. It is the lair of head-hunters, the homeland of the semi-civilized Dayaks. It is always there. It haunts me. I am tired of it and I hate it ever since I was a kid" (1:254). Simply put, the rainforest is emblematic of the primitive that threatens to engulf the civilized city-dweller on the other side of the Sarawak River. This "fear-hate relationship with the rainforest" (1:260) seems to dissipate once Yong is inside the rainforest, even though he continues to characterize the jungle as "primeval" and "prelapsarian" (1:240, 261). Yong instead becomes fascinated by wildlife, which is metonymically presented by the enthralling scene of the copulation of two white water snakes (1:240). Yong's idealization of the jungle as one which is deprived of any traces of human civilization is reminiscent of Marlow's comment: "We were wanderers on a prehistoric earth, on an earth that wore the aspect of an unknown planet. We could have fancied ourselves the first of men taking possession of an accursed inheritance to be subdued at the cost of profound anguish and of excessive toil" (Conrad, *Youth* 79). But unlike Conrad, Li stops short of rehearsing mid-nineteenth-century evolutionary discourses.

Despite superficially characterizing Borneo as a primitive heart of darkness, Li, like Conrad before him, subverts the conventional associations of light with goodness, truth, purity, and civilization and darkness with evil, death, depravity, and primitiveness.[21] Critics have offered numerous interpretations of Kurtz as the heart of darkness, ranging from the corruption of imperial policy, to moral vacancy (Kurtz is "hollow at the core" [Conrad, *Youth* 104]), to sexism, to miscegenation, to human sacrifice.[22] Marlow always imagines Kurtz as a voice, "the pulsating stream of light or the deceitful flow from the heart of an impenetrable darkness" (92). A few pages later, we realize that such a gift of persuasion enables Kurtz to author a report that concludes, "Exterminate all the brutes!" (95). Moreover, Marlow says that, as he enters the Intended's house, the following vision accompanies him of Kurtz as "a shadow insatiable of splendid appearances, of frightful realities; a shadow darker than the shadow of the night and draped nobly in the folds of a gorgeous eloquence" (121). Kurtz and Li's victimizers, whose physical whiteness is constantly underscored, are all gifted with eloquence and persuasiveness. More specifically, white pedophiles in Li's novel trap brown virgins with enticing and yet diabolic rhetoric, such as a sacrilegious pretext or a promising future abroad. In *The End of the River*, the penetration of would-be light comes in the form of rape rather than goodness or purity. Conrad's titular phrase is, in other words, repurposed to critique specific racial and gender oppression that lingers long after Indonesia gained independence from the Netherlands. Li's "heart of darkness" refers to white men's moral depravity but not the savagery of the native people, even though Li's somewhat racist poetics may sometimes suggest otherwise.

The End of the River directly indicts white men for their sexual exploitation of Indigenous women by also drawing upon Conrad's *Lord Jim*, specifically through the circulation of rumor and myth. In *Lord Jim*, Marlow rehearses many rumors surrounding the eponymous hero, most notably his whiteness and its supernatural associations, which are inherited by one of the victimizers in *The End of the River*. Marlow says that "In the midst of these dark-faced men, his stalwart figure in white apparel, the gleaming clusters of his fair hair, seemed to catch all the sunshine that trickled through the cracks [. . .]. He appeared like a creature not only of another kind but of another essence" (Conrad, *Lord Jim* 174). But Marlow quickly adds that, "Had they not seen [Jim] come up in a canoe they might have thought he had descended upon them from the clouds" (174). Marlow moreover recounts that the Indigenous people attribute supernatural powers to Jim owing to his possession of firearms (201). To this Jim replies "with an exasperated little laugh" that "What can you do with such silly beggars? They will sit up half the night talking bally rot, and the greater the lie the more they seem to like it" (201). Jim is further associated with a myth concerning an enormous, priceless, though probably unlucky emerald, a story that is "as old as the arrival of the first white men in the Archipelago; and the belief in it is so persistent that less than forty years ago there had been an official Dutch inquiry into the truth of it" (211). Marlow heard from the natives that Jim obtains it "partly by the exercise of his wonderful strength and partly by cunning" and that Jim is framed as "the ruler of a distant country, when he had fled instantly, arriving in Patusan in utmost distress but frightening the people by his extreme ferocity, which nothing seemed able to subdue" (211).

If Simpson is rumored to be an imperial hero in the lineage of Sir James Brooke, Aussie is widely known among the Indigenous people as *bapak* (the Malay word for father) and someone who can perform "enthralling magic tricks" to children and adults alike (Li, *River* 1:124, 130). As a white man who works for the Indonesian government and who frequents the tribes, Aussie recalls Jim's whiteness and associated privilege.[23] *Lord Jim* memorably opens with this portrayal of Jim: "He was *spotlessly neat*, apparelled in *immaculate white from shoes to hat*, and in the various Eastern ports where he got his living as ship-chandler's water-clerk he was very *popular*" (Conrad, *Lord Jim* 9; my emphasis). Yong introduces Aussie in extremely similar terms: "*I do not recall his real name*; I only remember that he was an Australian citizen, a white-haired lawyer in his 50s, an amicable white man who was *extremely popular* with kids. From his *spotlessly neat, creamy white* summer suit, he took out an abundance of candy, just like playing magic tricks" (Li, *River* 1:124; my emphasis).[24] Throughout the novel, Aussie always wears white shoes (1:202), sports a full head of white hair (1:206), and carries an aluminum suitcase (1:131). In addition to the fact that Jim and Aussie are noted for their whiteness, it is significant that both characters are only known respectively as "Lord Jim" and "*bapak* Aussie," names and honorific titles that are given by the Indigenous people and that ironically do not match their deeds. These names, which occlude their real identities, mythologize the characters as imperial heroes and benefactors of Indigenous people.

Moreover, Li's novel alternates between the celebratory discourse associated with Aussie and the stories of rape and abandonment by white men. For instance, Aussie lures an Iban girl called Iman to make love with him with his magic tricks and a promise for a better life in Australia but subsequently deserts her (1:198). The narratee, Zhu Ling, plays a crucial role in unveiling

Aussie's crimes by picking up incomplete storylines and eliciting more stories from the narrator (2:110–07). We learn that Aussie capitalizes on his job as a legal consultant for various tribes, which serves as a pretext for him to frequent the villages and prey upon girls (2:112). Iman's story is therefore taken to be iterative, representing the white men's broader exploitation of native girls. Another exemplary victim is Maria Aniah, who was impregnated by Father Pedro. Both Father Pedro and Aussie, not unlike Kurtz before them, wield compelling yet diabolical rhetoric. We learn that Father Pedro convinces everyone that Maria Aniah was bearing baby Jesus; for this reason, she was called "Madonna" (2:94, 105). Like all other raped women who die during labor or drown themselves along with their babies, she becomes a *pontianak*, a malevolent spirit whose sigh precedes the ghost.[25] A key figure in the second volume, Maria Aniah follows Yong all the way up to Batu Tiban and repeatedly tells him her suffering and fate, stories that he then recounts.

To a certain degree, the tales of Iman and Maria Aniah recall Jewel's unnamed mother's fragmented account of being abused and abandoned by white men in *Lord Jim*.[26] Jewel's educated, good-looking Dutch-Malay mother was born to a white high official, "one of the brilliantly endowed men who are not dull enough to nurse a success and whose careers so often end under a cloud" (Conrad, *Lord Jim* 167, 208). We can only sketch the following biography for her: after separating from Jewel's white biological father, she married Cornelius, a Malacca Portuguese, who was appointed a manager of Stein's trading post in Patusan solely because of her (167). She found companionship only in her daughter (208) since Cornelius "led her an awful life, stopping only short of actual ill-usage, for which he had not the pluck" (217). But this last point seems to be an understatement of Cornelius's abusive nature, judging by all his malicious undertakings in the novel and by the fact that he is barred from seeing his dying wife. Moreover, it seems that the daughter is bound to repeat the life of her mother, along with the regret and fear of being abused and deserted by white men. Marlow elliptically remarks, "I'm sure that the mother was as much of a woman as the daughter seemed to be," and that "there must have been confidences, not so much of fact, I suppose, as of innermost feeling—regrets—fears—warnings, no doubt: warnings that the younger did not fully understand till the elder was dead—and Jim came along. Then I am sure she understood much—not everything—the fear mostly it seems" (209). But even as Jewel tells Marlow that "you always leave us—for your own ends," she claims that "He [Jim] shall have no tears from me. Never, never. Not one tear. I will not! He went away from me as if I had been worse than death" (262). More significantly, Jewel is noted for her bravery and resourcefulness, making her a far cry from the victimized girls in *The End of the River*. Jewel, for example, tells Jim that she does not need him to kill Cornelius because "if she had not been sure he [Cornelius] was intensely wretched himself, she would have found the courage to kill him with her own hands" (218). Moreover, on several occasions she acts as Jim's strategist and protector, offering him useful advice about Patsan affairs and saving him from an attack in his sleep. She even commands the fort to prepare for an invasion from Brown by being in charge of the distribution of gunpowder and bullets (219, 224, 272–74). Nevertheless, the real names of Jewel and her mother as well as the bulk of their lives exceed narration. Strangely, Stein has little to offer, despite the fact that he "knew so many stories" and that Jewel stays at his house after Jim's death (208). By casting the Indigenous victims as *pontianaks* that constantly return to tell their stories, Li partially restores women's narrative space and voice, even when they are not portrayed as agents like Jewel.

In this essay, I have argued that Yong-Ping Li indicts white men for sexual abuse of Indigenous women by reworking the following Conradian elements: the trope of going upriver in the jungle, the title "heart of darkness" and related phrases, and the circulation of rumors and imperial myths. The "heart of darkness" that the narrator of *The End of the River* Yong probes is not so much the depth of the Borneo rainforest as the moral corruption of white men. Li contrasts Aussie's whiteness, a white speck reminiscent of Jim, and Borneo's darkness—more specifically the color of the Indigenous people and the dense, femininized, and mysterious rainforest—to overturn the conventional symbolic values of light and darkness. In so doing, Li underscores the white men's sexual exploitation of Indigenous women. Instrumental in bringing out this critique is the characters' obsession with storytelling, which Li draws from *Lord Jim*. Additionally, the suppressed narrative of sexual abuse and abandonment, glimpsed in Jewel's mother, is brought to full light through the *pontianaks*, which haunt Yong with their tales of suffering. Ultimately, just as Yong needs Zhu Ling to complete the story, so *The End of the River* demands that the reader decipher how it "writes back" to the Empire to tell the lost stories of sexual abuse.

NOTES

I wish to thank Brian Richardson, Christina Walter, and the anonymous readers for their feedback on the earlier version of this article.

1. Two of the few discussions are Erwan Zhang's essay on the Malay translations of *Gaspar Ruiz* and *Almayer's Folly* and Yoon-Wah Wong's chapters on Conrad's thematic and formal influence on Chinese writer Lao She in *Post-Colonial Chinese Literatures in Singapore and Malaysia*.

2. The Chinese title of the novel is 大河盡頭. There is no English translation of this novel; page numbers refer to the Chinese publications. All translations in this essay are my own.

3. In this essay, I do not focus on Christina's traumatic experience as a comfort woman—despite the fact that it also drives the overall narrative—because Li does not especially rework Conrad to portray it. The Japanese soldiers' sexual exploitation of women from nearby countries during the Second World War could indeed be considered a form of "heart of darkness," namely moral depravity. Nevertheless, except for this point, Li does not repurpose, for example, the trope of going upriver and "going mad," the imperial rhetoric of light penetrating darkness, or the oral transmission of rumors and (colonial) myths, to unfold Christina's past.

4. See for example Kim Tong Tee's entry on Li in *The Dictionary of Literary Biography*.

5. One might object that the novel does not represent Conrad's reception in Malaysia or Indonesia since Li did not identify as Malaysian and since the novel is mainly set in Indonesia and briefly in Sarawak in 1962 (namely, a year before the establishment of Malaysia). Indeed, in a 2009 interview with Yan-Ling Wu and Hui-Min Shi, Li claims that "I have never felt close to Malaysia in my entire life. I have never written about the Malay Peninsula, only about Borneo. [. . . .] It was only after Malaysia was established and I needed an identity that I obtained a Malaysian passport. But in my heart I couldn't think of myself as a citizen" (qtd. in Chan 66). Nevertheless, Li later thinks of himself as both a Malaysian Sinophone writer and a Taiwanese writer in a 2015 interview with Chia-Cian Ko (Ko 266). Moreover, I follow many critics, whom I mention in this essay, in considering Li a writer of Malaysian Sinophone literature. Since my focus is on Li's Conradian reworkings, I do not have space here to recapitulate the copious scholarship on Li's anxiety about his cultural identity. Instead, I refer English-speaking readers to the work of, for example, Cheow Thia Chan, Alison Groppe, and Chia-Rong Wu.

6. Depending on the book analyzed and the critical lens employed, different interpretations emerge of Li's engagement with the Chinese literary tradition. As Min-Xu Zhan outlines, there are four paradigms in the studies of Li: 1) the "Chinese paradigm" in the 1980s that foregrounds Li's Sinophilia; 2) the "Malaysian Sinophone paradigm" in the 1990s when scholars such as Kien Ket Lim, Kim-Chew Ng, and Kim Tong Tee draw upon diaspora studies to argue that Li's Sinophilia stems from his diasporic identity; 3) the "Borneo paradigm" in the 2010s that focuses on cultural hybridity in *The Snow Falls in Clouds* and *The End of the River*; and 4) most recently, the turn, initiated by Zhan, to analyze Li's writings of Taiwan and examine the neglected issue of Li's Taiwanese identity. See Zhan's essay collected in Ko (139–40).

7. My focus here is on the comparison between Conrad's and Li's deployment of cartography as a critique of colonialism and as a means of presenting alternative worldviews, while Cheow Thia Chan's is on Li's "negotia[tion] of a bifurcated self-positionality that straddles both Taiwanese and Malaysian Chinese-language literary systems" (64).

8. Li in his preface to the simplified Chinese edition of *The End of the River* reproduces this following quote from the beginning of the traditional Chinese edition: Yong asks Zhu Ling to "Open a big world map. Isn't there an island lying above the equator at 115°E, 0°N, south of the South China Sea and north of the Java sea [. . .]?" (1:xii)

9. The scholarship on this trope is copious. See, for example, Marianne DeKoven, Jeremy Hawthorn, Padmini Mongia, and Marianna Torgovnick.

10. Li's narratee has a more substantial role than those in the Marlow narratives since she elicits stories from the narrator. Zhu Ling is moreover comparable to Marlow and Lingard as

a transtextual character, which is defined by Cedric Watts as "one which exists in, across, and between two or more texts" ("Transtextual Narratives" 61). It is unclear whether Li was directly inspired by Conrad's transtextual characters, but both authors use this device as a bridge or synecdoche to invoke a previous tale without recounting it in full. Zhu Ling reminds the reader about Yong's first trip to the rainforest told earlier (Li, *River* 2:40). She even refers to the story about one of Yong's teachers who has gone missing in the rainforest (previously told in *The Snow Falls in Clouds*) when the teacher's head is on display in one of the longhouses (1:129).

11. For a discussion of Conrad's imperial storytellers, see, for example, Jennifer Wellman.

12. Yong tells us that he was a fifteen-year-old in 1962, having just finished junior high school. The change in Yong's curriculum may refer to the adoption of Sarawak-centric textbooks by the English-medium schools in 1954 and by Chinese-medium schools in 1958–60. According to Ooi Keat Gin, these textbooks were written with the aim of rectifying the lack of local content in the British and Chinese textbooks that English- and Chinese-medium schools respectively adopted, and to further pave way for the creation of a national education system (50).

13. More generally, Conrad's Tuan Putih (white lord) figures are composites of adventurers like James Brooke and the residents who ruled in the outposts generally without the intervention of the colonial state (Yeow 83).

14. The obituary for Brooke in *The Illustrated London News* (July 4, 1868) noted how "the new English rajah" began his reign in 1841 "with the good will of all his native subjects, whose welfare he carefully studied to promote" (qtd. in Hampson 4–5).

15. See, for example, Christopher GoGwilt's discussion in chapter 3 of *The Invention of the West*.

16. It is unclear to what extent those depictions of Indigenous people indicate Yong's own attitude toward the Indigenous people. Yong should be familiar with the Indigenous cultures because there were racially mixed (Chinese and Indigenous) communities in Sarawak. His portrayals of the Indigenous people may therefore present less his own idea of the Indigenous cultures and more of the purported view of Western visitors. Additionally, at one point, Yong claims that he is not really interested in the Indigenous customs, or more specifically the longhouses, because he has already visited one before (Li, *River* 1:126). Nevertheless, Yong's repeated investment in the women's breasts and the men's tattoos and *palang* throughout the novel seems to contradict this claim.

17. A palang (ampallang) refers to a male genital piercing that penetrates horizontally through the entire glans of the penis.

18. This conflation, commonly seen in the scholarship on Li, may result from the pervasive autobiographical parallels between Yong and Li, parallels that Li himself underscores in the interviews. Yong and Li were born as Chinese settlers in Kuching in 1947. Both went to Chinese elementary and middle schools; moved to Taiwan for college and the U.S. for graduate schools; and settled in the eastern part of Taiwan later in life. In addition to having the same general trajectory of life and experience, the names of the narrator and the author contain the character, Yong (永).

19. For an insightful analysis of Conrad's characterizations of the Africans, see Hunt Hawkins. According to Hawkins, Marlow praises the Africans for their energy, vitality, and dignity, even though all the examples are undercut by phrases that continue to associate the

Africans with the uncivilized. Overlooked by Chinua Achebe is Marlow's recognition of the humanity of the Africans. By remarking that drums in Africa have "as profound a meaning as the sound of bells in a Christian country," Marlow sees that the Africans are kin to him because they also have reverence (Hawkins 339).

20. For the mass conversion to Christianity among the Dayak people during the mid-twentieth century, see Victor King, *The Peoples of Borneo* (142–43), Jan Sihar Aritonavy and Karel Steenbrink, eds., *A History of Christianity in Indonesia* (499–509), and the entry on Dayak in *The Encyclopedia Britannica*.

21. See for example Terry Collits's *Postcolonial Conrad* (111), Tom Henthorne's *Conrad's Trojan Horse* (123–27), and Watts's *Conrad's Heart of Darkness* (8–9).

22. See Straus, Torgovnick, and Firchow, respectively.

23. I would note that Aussie's whiteness does not have the same implications as Jim's whiteness. Numerous critics have discussed that Conrad's Jim engages with the late-nineteenth-century stereotype of the English gentleman. As the ideal type of the Anglo-Saxon race and of the administrative officers of the Empire, the English gentleman connotes manliness, athleticism, heroism, and Christianity (Puxan-Oliva 345).

24. The original Chinese phrase of "spotlessly neat, creamy white summer suit" is 光鮮筆挺的乳白夏季西裝, which can be literally translated as "a creamy white summer suit that is brilliant in color and clean and ironed" (Li, *River* 1:124)

25. For the *pontianak* figure see, for example, King (242) and Tan (160). *Pontianak* is not a female vampire, contrary to what one of the minor characters claims in the novel (Li, *River* 2:63).

26. One may object that, since Jewel and her mother are mixed-race, they do not represent the white men's sexual abuse of Indigenous women. Nevertheless, Robert Hampson writes that Jewel and her mother suggest the malign replication of narrative for colonized women, a narrative of exploitation and desertion by European men (134). Moreover, Andrew Francis remarks that "Jewel's mother's marriage to another Eurasian, Cornelius, is down in terms of the colonial social scale" (101). Jewel and her mother therefore exemplify the broader colonial sexual exploitation of mixed-race and Indigenous women. Such an issue continued to exist in 1962, even after Indonesia declared independence from the Netherlands, since Li's Indigenous characters are raped by white colonialist figures.

WORKS CITED

Allen, Jerry. *The Sea Years of Joseph Conrad*. Doubleday, 1965.

Aritonang, Jan Sihar, and Karel Steenbrink, eds. *A History of Christianity in Indonesia*. Brill, 2008.

Brantlinger, Patrick. *Rule of Darkness: British Literature and Imperialism, 1830–1914*. Cornell University Press, 1990.

Bronstein, Michaela. *Out of Context: The Uses of Modernist Fiction*. Oxford University Press, 2018.

Chan, Cheow Thia. "Indigeneity, Map-Mindedness, and World-Literary Cartography: The Poetics and Politics of Li Yongping's Transregional Chinese Literary Production." *Modern Chinese Literature and Culture*, vol. 30, no. 1, 2018, pp. 63–86.

Collits, Terry. *Postcolonial Conrad: Paradoxes of Empire*. Routledge, 2005.

Conrad, Joseph. *The Nigger of the "Narcissus": A Tale of the Sea*. Edited by Allan H. Simmons, Cambridge University Press, 2017.
———. *Lord Jim: A Tale*. Edited by J.H. Stape and Ernest W. Sullivan, Cambridge University Press, 2012.
———. *Youth, Heart of Darkness, The End of the Tether*. Edited by Owen Knowles, Cambridge University Press, 2010.
"Dayak." *Encyclopedia Britannica*. Accessed 1 July 2020.
Dryden, Linda. *Joseph Conrad and the Imperial Romance*. St. Martin's Press, 2000.
DeKoven, Marianne. *Rich and Strange: Gender, History, Modernism*. Princeton University Press, 1991.
Firchow, Peter. *Envisioning Africa: Racism and Imperialism in Conrad's Heart of Darkness*. University of Kentucky Press, 2000.
Francis, Andrew. *Culture and Commerce in Conrad's Asian Fiction*. Cambridge University Press, 2015.
Gin, Ooi Keat. "Education in Sarawak during the Period of Colonial Administration, 1946–1963." *Journal of the Malaysian Branch of the Royal Asiatic Society*, vol. 64, no. 2, 1990, pp. 35–68.
GoGwilt, Christopher. *The Invention of the West: Joseph Conrad and the Double-Mapping of Europe and Empire*. Stanford University Press, 1995.
Griffith, John. *Joseph Conrad and the Anthropological Dilemma: "Bewildered Traveler."* Oxford University Press, 1995.
Groppe, Alison. *Sinophone Malaysian Literature: Not Made in China*. Cambria Press, 2013.
———. "Writer-Wanderer Li Yongping and Chinese Malaysian Literature." *A New Literary History of Modern China*, edited by David Der-Wei Wang, Harvard University Press, 2017, pp. 906–11.
Hampson, Robert. *Cross-Cultural Encounters in Joseph Conrad's Malay Fiction*. Palgrave, 2000.
Hawkins, Hunt. "*Heart of Darkness* and Racism." *Heart of Darkness*, 5th ed., edited by Paul B. Armstrong, Norton, 2017.
Hawthorn, Jeremy. *Sexuality and the Erotic in the Fiction of Joseph Conrad*. Continuum, 2007.
Horton, William. "Comfort Women." *The Encyclopedia of Indonesia in the Pacific War*, edited by Peter Post, et al., Brill, 2010.
King, Victor T. *The Peoples of Borneo*. Blackwell, 1993.
Ko, Chia-Cian, ed. 見山又是山：李永平研究 [*Yong-Ping Li Studies*]. Ryefield, 2017.
Li, Yong-Ping. 李永平 大河盡頭上卷：溯流. [*The End of the River, Volume 1: Going Upstream*] Renmin Press, 2012.
———. 大河盡頭下卷：山. [*The End of the River, Volume 2: The Mountain*] Renmin Press, 2012.
———. 海東青：台北的一則寓言 [*Haidong Blues: A Fable of Taipei*]. 聯合文學 [Lianhe wenxue], 1992.
———. "Interview." *The Beijing News*, 2012. http://www.bjnews.com.cn/book/2012/05/19/199850.html. Accessed June 20, 2020.
———. 吉陵春秋. [*Retribution: The Jiling Chronicles*]. Translated by Howard Goldblatt and Sylvia Li-Chun Lin, Columbia University Press, 2003.

———. 雨雪霏霏：婆羅洲童年記事 [*The Snow Falls in Clouds: Recollections of a Borneo Childhood*]. Ryefield, 2013.

Mongia, Padmini. "'Ghosts of the Gothic': Spectral Women and Colonized Spaces in *Lord Jim*." *The Conradian*, vol. 17, no. 2, 1993, pp. 1–16.

———. "Empire, Narrative, and the Feminine in *Lord Jim* and *Heart of Darkness*." *Under Postcolonial Eyes: Joseph Conrad after Empire*, edited by Gail Fincham and Myrtle Hooper, University of Cape Town Press, 1996, pp. 120–32.

Ng, Kim-Chew. "流離的婆羅洲之子與他的母親、父親" ["The Exiled Son of Borneo and His Parents"]. 見山又是山：李永平研究 [*Yong-Ping Li Studies*], edited by Chia-Cian Ko, Ryefield, 2017, pp. 55–94.

———. "石頭與女鬼—論《大河盡頭》中的象徵交換與死亡" [On the Death and the Symbolic Exchange in *Where the Big River Ends*]. 台灣文學研究學報 [*Taiwan wenxue yanjiu xuebao*], vol. 14, 2012, pp. 241–63.

Puxan-Oliva, Marta. "Racial Stereotypes as Narrative Forms: Staging the English Gentleman in Joseph Conrad's *Lord Jim*." *Journal of Narrative Theory*, vol. 45, no. 3, 2015, pp. 333–69.

Sun, Zi-Ping. "An Interview with Yong-Ping Li." 2010. http://web.mit.edu/ccw/li-yongping/files/2010%20Interview-%20Translation.pdf. Accessed June 20, 2020.

Straus, Nina Pelikan. "The Exclusion of the Intended from Secret Sharing in Conrad's *Heart of Darkness*." *Joseph Conrad's Heart of Darkness: A Casebook*, edited by Gene Moore, Oxford University Press, 2004, pp. 197–217.

Tan, Kenneth Paul. "Pontianaks, Ghosts and the Possessed: Female Monstrosity and National Anxiety in Singapore Cinema." *Asian Studies Review*, vol. 34, pp. 151–70.

Tee, Kim Tong. "Li Yongping." *The Dictionary of Literary Biography, Volume 370: Chinese Fiction Writers, 1950–2000*, edited by Thomas Moran and Ye (Dianna) Xu, Gale, 2013, pp. 149–56.

Torgovnick, Marianna. *Gone Primitive: Savage Intellects, Modern Lives*. University of Chicago Press, 1990.

Watts, Cedric. "Conrad's Covert Plots and Transtextual Narratives." *Critical Quarterly*, vol. 24, no. 3, 1982, pp. 53–64.

———. *Conrad's Heart of Darkness: A Critical and Contextual Discussion*. Rodopi, 2012.

Wellman, Jennifer. "Orality and Outcasts: Joseph Conrad and the Imperial Narrator." *Conradiana*, no. 45, no. 1, 2013, pp. 5–29.

White, Andrea. *Joseph Conrad and the Adventure Tradition: Constructing and Deconstructing the Imperial Subject*. Cambridge University Press, 1993.

Wong, Yoon-Wah. *Post-Colonial Chinese Literatures in Singapore and Malaysia*. National University of Singapore Press, 2002.

Wu, Chia-Rong. *Supernatural Sinophone Taiwan and Beyond*. Cambria Press, 2016.

Yeow, Agnes. *Conrad's Eastern Vision: A Vain and Floating Appearance*. Palgrave, 2009.

Zhang, Erwan. "Conrad and the Formation of National Identity: The Malay Translations of 'Gaspar Ruiz' and *Almayer's Folly*." *Studia Neophilologica*, vol. 85, supp. 1, 2013, pp. 69–81.

The True Self as Social Solidarity in Conrad's *The Secret Sharer* and *The Shadow-Line*

ERIK ROBB THOMPSON

THE CATHOLIC UNIVERSITY OF KOREA

Keywords: Joseph Conrad, D.W. Winnicott, creative mimesis, true self and false self, Rene Girard

ABSTRACT

Seeking to contribute to the recent scholarly work on Girardian mimesis, this article adds a Winnicottian dimension in the form of a dialectic between false and true selves to an analysis of two works by Joseph Conrad. Scholars such as Nidesh Lawtoo and Martha Reineke elaborate, widen, and interrogate what Girard himself has written about positive mimesis. This project will build on Reineke's work of bringing Rene Girard and D.W. Winnicott together and apply the central claim about creative mimesis to the social dynamic and the liminal crises experienced by young captains in *The Secret Sharer* and *The Shadow-Line*. *The Secret Sharer* shows a novice captain's creative individualism moving in the direction of group solidarity, but only to the extent that he forms a coterie with his psychological double. The discussion of *The Shadow-Line* details how another new captain's initial rejection of the false self, coupled with his inability to control only through a mindset of heroic individualism, results in a socially situated true self in solidarity with crew members. In this way, the novella completes the dialectic by showing communal solidarity to be the result of a shift from destructive mimesis (rejection of the false self) to creative mimesis (acceptance of the false self as a delimiter to creative individualism and true self life) in the relationships with others. This article will conclude by connecting the above claims to Conrad's aesthetic ideas.

Conrad often depicts individuals alienated from reality. The captain from *The Secret Sharer*, Jim of *Lord Jim*, and the narrator of *Under Western Eyes* all show signs of being true to themselves by remaining remote from others. A recent biographer of Conrad notes how Conrad's characters "struggle with displacement, alienation and despair. Seventeen commit suicide" (Jasanoff 52). These depictions have led to pessimistic readings of Conrad. According to Ian Watt, Conrad's Marlow resignedly finds the partial remedy for this condition of alienation in a "saving lie" in which "untruth as a condition of life" becomes "life furthering" (246). Less pessimistically, D.W. Winnicott, a twentieth-century psychoanalytical theorist who also explored the problem of alienation from reality, described it in terms of true and false selves, a theory first laid out in his paper, "Ego Distortion in Terms of True and False Self" (1960). While false selves "exist out of touch with the subjective world and with the creative approach to fact" (Winnicott, *Playing* 67), the false self nevertheless sometimes acts as a necessary defense mechanism for survival in a social world. The true self or the primary self is the source of an individual's spontaneity, creativity, and the feeling of aliveness, and in a social sense is seen in a subject's creative participation in a culture. Considering Conrad's fiction in terms of Winnicott's conceptual framework helps us notice a more positive psychology, and even potentially therapeutic value, than it has often been granted. But the question remains how the two modes of being relate to each other, especially in light of the problems associated with identifying and determining the difference between the false and true self.

Seeking to contribute to scholarship that integrates twentieth-century psychological theory with twenty-first-century mimetic studies of Conrad, this article adds a Winnicottian dimension in following Martha Reineke's idea of "creative mimesis" within transitional spaces to analyze the question of how the two types of selves are to be read in two works by Joseph Conrad, *The Secret Sharer* and *The Shadow-Line* (Reineke 83).[1] Reineke and other mimetic theorists such as Nidesh Lawtoo, Anne Belford Ulanov, and Pablo Bandera elaborate, widen, and interrogate Rene Girard's theory of positive mimesis present in his work since his *Things Hidden Since the Foundation of the World* (1987). This project draws from Reineke's bringing Girard and Winnicott together in order to illuminate a Winnicottian understanding of solidarity in *The Secret Sharer* and *The Shadow-Line*. Katherine Rising's reading of MacWhirr as a false-self type of captain in *Typhoon*, citing Winnicott's theory and terms, constitutes the whole of existing scholarship that looks at Conrad from a Winnicottian perspective. Rising's emphasis on the false self in Conrad, with MacWhirr as efficacious but impoverished in cultural and social life and incapable of symbolic thinking, stands to be expanded to include the "true self," which is the other side of Winnicott's idea of a healthy psyche. Differing from Freud, Winnicott places more emphasis on the study of health in general, and on the relationship between health and creativity (which Freud famously disparaged as infantile and governed by a sublimation of the pleasure principle), particularly in terms of mediated object relations. In focusing on health and creativity, Winnicott builds on Melanie Klein's object relations theory, which is more amenable than Freud's theory to a less rigidly masculinist understanding of human development (Freud 294–97; Klein 42–70).[2]

In Reineke's concept of creative mimesis, desire for the object is socially construed; it is never an "I" that stands in an exclusive relationship to an object of desire, rather, desire is always situated in a web of human relationships in which social participation defines object relations.[3] Creative mimesis offers an alternative to acquisitive mimesis, wherein the threat of others' influences results in escalating panic and the eventual scapegoating of social outsiders to achieve a social stasis.[4] For Reineke, social relationships do not necessarily result in unresolved antipathy, necessitating a sacrificial victim. Rather, cooperation is made possible by a nurturing figure that Winnicott calls a "good enough mother" (*Playing* 13), who allows the subject to express himself socially through her example of ontological sharing, rather than setting the stage for conflicts centered on a model who comes to depend on a rival's attention in their "quest" for the model's being (Reineke 83). Reineke recognizes in Winnicott's concept of a mediating "good enough mother"

> A gift that "woos us into shared love" and is expressed as agape, mothering initially entails full responsiveness to our desires. But slowly, as the human subject is held in this love, the one who is mothering that subject draws back, "making room for objects that do not immediately answer our imagining of them and thus making room for our aggression." Holding fast in the face of destructiveness, the one who expresses agape facilitates the transformation of aggression into imaginative work and creative living. (Reineke 89)

Ultimately, for Reineke, "Mimetic desire is desire for God" as the source of being (80). For this article on Conrad, mimetic desire is desire for God's modernist ersatz found in the creative and cultural energies already present in what Winnicott refers to as the "cultural pool," defined as "the inherited tradition, [. . .] the common pool of humanity" (*Playing* 133).

A contrasting type of positive mimesis is found in Conrad critic Nidesh Lawtoo's *The Phantom of the Ego*, where he posits a dichotomy in modernist novels between "enthusiasm" and "distance," enthusiasm being a result of mimetic unconsciousness and distance being the anti-mimetic instincts acquired through experience and education that override the natural impulse to imitate others when so inspired (106, 142). In terms of Conrad's *The Shadow-Line*, Lawtoo asks, how does the narrator-captain not succumb to the mimetic challenges of first mate Burns? By distancing himself from his enthusiasm, is the answer. Similar to Girard, Lawtoo criticizes psychoanalytic critics who reduce group psychology to the analysis of the ego, which appears to put him at odds with Reineke's attempt to bring a pediatrist-turned-psychoanalytic-theorist, Winnicott, and an anthropologist-turned-literary-theorist and theologian, Girard, together. For example, Lawtoo maintains that ego-focused critics fail to recognize that in Leggatt's account of his crime in *The Secret Sharer*, panic generates madness that disrupts the systems of relations upon which the ship as "anthropocene" rests (*Shadow* 48). Lawtoo further claims it is a mistake to identify Leggatt as an elitist egoist, given his ethic of choosing to save the maximum number of people through the murder of one person. Hence, Lawtoo's remedy for how mimetic madness is overcome is also different from Reineke's: a socially and environmentally situated individual, who, by training and profession, can intuit the systemic implications of a threat of the contagiousness of panic, and is also in a position to evaluate and effectively counter it. In Lawtoo's reading, "'Thou shalt not kill' can be transgressed on the prospect of attaining the greater good for the wider ecology of humans interacting in nature (72). Similarly, in the case of *Typhoon*, and different from Rising's account of MacWhirr as a false-self "normotic" (124), Lawtoo claims the novella demonstrates that MacWhirr's training qua instinct is the means by which catastrophe is avoided.

Agreeing with the emphasis on systems, this article adds to Lawtoo's work by showing how nurturing characters, Leggatt from *The Secret Sharer* and Ransome from *The Shadow Line*, provide the personal security for the narrators' healthy, albeit transient, reframing of a destructive type of imitation, "enthusiasm" in Lawtoo's terms, that sidesteps the panic induced by the mimetic unconscious. These figures are present in a subject's transitional or liminal space in Winnicott and in a mimetic triangle in Girard. Even as adults, Winnicott claims, such spaces with an adequate mother figure as an integral part give an individual the security to creatively project his or her fantasies onto a transitional object, existing in a cultural gray area between the psyche and real world. Such objects act as stepping stones to psychological health—defined by the ability to behave creatively in a social sphere.[5] Specifically, the subject forms the illusion of having created an object found in the outside world that is under his control, and the mother figure accepts that paradox by not challenging the subject as to whether they "created" this object or indeed simply "found" what was already there in the environment ("Ego Distortion" 145). Hence, what Lawtoo refers to as distance from madness Reineke sees as a socially transformed primary creativity that allows imitation to become creative instead of a contagious spiral of madness and panic.

In *The Secret Sharer* and *The Shadow-Line*, Leggatt and Ransome precipitate a dialectical process between a pursuit of true selves, manifested as a fear of dependency on others, and the threat of an enveloping false-self, manifested as the need to comply with the demands of reality, in the inexperienced captain-narrators. The dialectic can be plotted as follows: the unnamed captain-narrators in both texts both have nervous breakdowns on board the ships they command. Under the auspices of an attentive figure setting an example for a different type of mimesis, they give themselves over to near-madness before they find a way to be both creative and compliantly dutiful (a non-defensive form of the false self) in the reality of social life on a sailing ship which is the product of the dialectic. This solution is less pronounced in *The Secret Sharer*, in which the narrator's predicament is overcome by taking on the persona of an idealized alter-ego figure. In both cases, crises at sea in transitional spaces resulting in the specter of a destructive madness are transformed into creative mimesis, which in turn allow the true-self narrators to enter into a provisional creative solidarity with others. In taking psychological possession of the ship, the captain in *The Secret Sharer*, as I will discuss, shows psychological development to the extent that he forms a coterie with his psychological double. In *The Shadow-Line*, the title itself indicating a liminal space, another newly-appointed captain's rejection of the false self, coupled with his inability to control events alone through a mindset of aristocratic individualism, results in his socially situated true self. In this way, the novella completes the dialectic by showing community to be the result of a shift from destructive mimesis (a self-defeating rejection of the false self) to creative mimesis in the relationships among the members of the crew. As a contrasting example, the search for the true self in *The Secret Sharer* will be analyzed next.

THE SEARCH FOR THE TRUE SELF IN
THE SECRET SHARER

Just as the false self embodies "a particular drive to be normal" (Rising 124), so the captain-narrator of *The Secret Sharer* embodies a romanticized version of a true-self mode of behavior at odds with social forces that seeks social distance from others in the process of his assuming command of the ship. With such a mindset, the narrator embarks on his first command in a state of deep uncertainty and ambivalence about himself, his crew, and even the geography at the mouth of a river in the Gulf of Siam, where they await favorable winds to begin their journey home. An excessively one-sided true self is seen in the captain-narrator's inherent instability as an individualistic Romantic hero seeking to safeguard his autonomy. The Girardian point to be highlighted is that at the outset the narrator appears already to be caught in the double bind of a mimetic crisis. He feels himself an imposter beset by the influences of others, presumably the examples of other captains in the lore of the merchant fleet, and is intent on maintaining the primacy of self at all costs even as he dons the socially-determined title of captain. The model in such a mimetic triangle feels as though imitators may rob them of their being, and therefore seeks to escape their influence by overemphasizing their unique qualities, which are actually those of a model. As Reineke observes, drawing on the work of Ann Belford Ulanov, a Union Theological Seminary professor and practicing psychoanalyst, it is at this stage when the true self is threatened by external forces that Winnicott's concept of transitional space, also at times a kind of "mad" intermediariness, resembles the inherent instability of Girard's mimetic triangle. One possible result of this crisis is the potential for a pathological form of the false self as the defensive response at any stage to the fear of the "loss of being" (Reineke 91). According to Ulanov,

> Without transforming ruthless aggression into the creative unconscious imagination, we lose the space between fantasy and reality and between ourselves and others; for then *we fear dependence*. We pull back from risking the dependence necessary to achieve it. [. . .] the [greater the] failure to meet our dependence [. . .] the greater the danger we sustain—psychosis or borderline functioning. We manufacture a false self to contain the yawning gap that did not grow, the aggression that would not be transformed [. . . .] We build defenses in reaction to imaginary attacks from without or from within. (118)

Creating this space separating fantasy and reality, self and others, requires a transformation of aggression into creative living. For Reineke and Ulanov, this is achieved through the sacred form of sometimes violent or anti-social play through which an individual learns that the source of selfhood lies in the sharing of the plenitude of being. In contrast, Lawtoo refers to this process as a "patho(-)logical lesson," a sidestepping of the "pathological" aspects of mimesis through an understanding of the cycles of mimetic violence gained through experience or a meta-rational diagnosis of its deleterious effects (*Shadow* 104).[6] For Lawtoo, when Leggatt acts and does not think in a crisis, we can see his act of violence serving as a model of an effective anti-mimetic defense against mutinous panic during a typhoon. In Leggatt's account, others, including the captain of the *Sephora*, were panicking; he was not. However, at the level of character, Leggatt's role in preventing the narrator's descent into a false-self fear of dependence should not only be limited to a cognitive diagnostic of the forces of mimesis.

The narrator's own depiction of his liminality, both psychological and geological, it must be said, already suggests his need for transforming aggression into the creative unconscious. As Mark Larabee has shown in his work on Conrad's imperialistic cartography, liminality is central to the story's physical and psychological imperatives, as "it explores the themes of solitude vs. community and self vs. other" (488). At the start of the captain's psychological journey, the reader encounters him pondering the divisions between land and sea, river and ocean, the enveloping jungle on the land and the imposing structure of a pagoda, and above all, divisions between himself, his ship and "the disturbing sounds" of the "voices, footsteps" of his crew (Conrad, *Sharer* 8). He apprehensively notes to himself how unknown he is to the rest of the crew: "All these people had been together for eighteen months and my position was that of stranger [. . .] and the truth must be told, I was somewhat of a stranger to myself" (8). The novice captain's behavior during this period when he seeks to shore up his sense of self suggests untransformed aggression and a fear of the false self.[7] This is seen in that he does not welcome his discovery of human presence in the form of the *Sephora* anchored in the otherwise abandoned solitude of his new command: "With all that multitude of celestial bodies staring down at one, the comfort of quiet communion with her was gone for good" (8). The detection a few lines earlier of the masts of a ship is resolved here into a subjective transference of menace to the outer world at large—as incursion into his private relationship with his ship.[8] Feeling trapped, he senses "sneering" in the "quivering lips" of his second mate reacting to a simple question, and in his scornful judgments of the first mate, whom he ridicules for earnestly over-speculating about everything "down to a miserable scorpion" that managed to drown itself in an inkwell (8–9). Nevertheless, at the outset, aboard his new command, despite the apprehensive atmosphere, the narrator has the luxury of time to assert himself and lash out against the external world in a manner of his choosing if he is to take control of the ship, himself, and his crew.

To that end, he begins a series of actions that readers have variously found irresponsible, disingenuous, and criminal.[9] Stanley Renner discerns a Nietzschean influence when Conrad's captain flaunts conventional morality and obeys his own instincts. If that is accurate, then for this argument that a Winnicottian analysis reveals the limits of the results of such an influence, this narrator-captain rejects the false-self role of following a conventional form of ascetic morality based on twenty centuries of "the law" (Renner 160). As a morally transgressing captain seeking to bolster his true-self mode of command, then, the narrator disturbs the peace and conventional thinking of those on his ship with irregular orders and departures from business as usual. The first such action he performs is to give his crew a break by allowing them to sleep while he takes the first watch on deck. The first and second mates don't know how to react to this unusual departure from protocol, but they somewhat confusedly comply with the order. This also gives the captain-narrator a chance to take stock of and project himself onto the ship, which like everything in this story is located in a liminal psychic space where the question of whether it is the narrator's command or the crew's is intertwined with the ship's physical presence.

Out of this space, seemingly, emerges his secret sharer, the fugitive Leggatt. A potential model in a destructive mimetic triangle, he may also play the role of a Winnicottian "good enough mother" that makes possible the captain's transforming of aggression and allowing of dependence so that a compliance to the demands of reality and social standards and true-self creative fantasy can coexist. From a more general point of view, Daphna Erdinast-Vulcan rightly notes that the figure of Leggatt seems prepared from the outset to "play on the assumed doubleness" arrived at through an accidental intimacy with the narrator (455). From the narrator's perspective, Leggatt's appearing to meet the captain's subjective creative impulses halfway leaves unanswered whether the second self is created by the narrator's need for such a self or was found in the very real visitation from the outside world in the form of an escaped murderer, to whom the captain has given refuge. So long as Leggatt's status is left unresolved, as transitional object he has symbolic potential for the captain. If resolved, the transitional space would devolve into a false-self submission to social reality—Leggatt's person is determined by the facts of his physical presence alone—or, on the other hand, into a true-self solipsism—Leggatt is a fantasy figure created by the captain. In the latter case, the captain remains impervious to or overly threatened by influences from the outside world.[10] Because the good-enough mother, Leggatt, allows this question in regards to the status of his own body to remain open, the captain is free to play a dangerous game with the person of Leggatt, as he clothes him in his own sleeping costume, lies with him in the same bunk, and conspires on his behalf to allow him to flee from justice in the manner of a fantasy taken from a "boy's adventure tale" (Conrad, *Sharer* 35). He gives himself leave to identify with Leggatt because it is as though he has created what appeared out of nowhere in the mirror of the sea, suddenly finding Leggatt "as though [he] had faced [his] own reflection in the depths" (14).

This is the point when his captaincy construed as a transitional space under the auspices of an indulgent good-enough mother becomes apparent in that he permits himself behavior that tests out a relationship with reality, even as he becomes increasingly estranged from the crew and wonders if they will discover his unlawful acts. His questionable behavior comes to a head when he misleads and lies to Leggatt's Captain Archbold from the *Sephora*, who comes aboard in a legal capacity to find the fugitive. From there, the story quickly descends into an aestheticized Poe-like flirtation with madness, characterized by a highly polarized search for a true-self mode of existence. In *The Secret Sharer*, as in Poe's stories of doubles, there is much initial anxiety in response to his secret, illicit actions:

> The Sunday quietness of the ship was against us; the stillness of air and water around her was against us; the elements, the men were against us—everything was against us in our secret relationship; time itself—for this could not go on forever. The very trust of Providence was, I suppose, denied to his guilt. Shall I confess this thought cast me down very much? (29)

An assessment of the uses of madness in a mimetic crisis is finally what is at stake in this self-imposed drama, in which the narrator feels it is "very much like being mad, only it was worse because one was aware of it" (23). He presses on to the brink of insanity, again resembling a mad narrator in a story by Poe, at times gloating in his aiding his fugitive double by inviting others like the ship's steward and Captain Archbold to thoroughly search his quarters. Conrad takes this Romantic trope of madness and the psychological double to rhetorically excessive lengths, which, according to Erdinast-Vulcan, "is a symptom of the narrator's need to stake out a spurious territory of selfhood" (452). In terms of the captain's actions within the narration rather than the narration itself, more than an exercise in aesthetic uses of language to defer a sense of reality, the novella shows that his need for selfhood based on fantasy projections creates the conditions within an intimate separate space from which the captain can act rashly to test out new relationships with objects from the outside world.

Even as he is touched by the immorality of his actions, the increasing intimacy with Leggatt affords him the security for such actions by which he can begin to stem the threat of destructive mimesis he felt at the onset of the voyage. During his time with Leggatt, the captain no longer feels as if he deserves the protection of divine providence, for he believes his aiding a murderer disqualifies him from such help. Nor does he look to luck or chance to save him, "for what favorable accident could be expected?" (Conrad, *Sharer* 30) Against divine, natural, and human foes, there are "the only two strangers on board," who believe in their human connection more than in traditional morality (30). Within the first-person narration that is in itself a reflection of the divide between self and world, the persona of Leggatt seems also to function as the captain's psychological foray into the outside world, with Leggatt characterized as a rugged character who suddenly jumps ship or murders an impudent sailor in a fit of anger. The captain's own fugitive status leads him to sympathize with such a projected-upon other's more dramatic plight, and to conform himself to this new presence, wryly regarding him as an uncanny extension of himself. It amounts to this: from the womblike space of his cabin, the captain can venture forth and begin "to make the acquaintance of his ship" (30), for as he states, "I was not wholly alone with my command; for there was that stranger in my cabin" (31). Not communicating restores greater psychological balance after too much withering false-self social compliance, but as Winnicott confirms, "The child is alone only in the presence of someone" (*Playing* 130). The lone narrator's voice mirrors another's, as the narrator's increasingly does Leggatt's: initially he too self-consciously gives orders to his first-mate; then at the high point of his identification with Leggatt, moments before seeing his hat floating in the sea, "his tone had a borrowed loudness"; and at the end, after recognizing the flesh and blood of his second self, symbolized by the floating hat, his orders sound a note of confidence in their brevity and "low voice" (40, 42). His severing himself at the end from the free swimmer may be read, in the terms presented here, as pointing to a gradually increasing ability to distinguish his voice from Leggatt's. Albert Guerard also saw Leggatt as a symbol who helps the captain "overcome his necessary but egoistic identification with Leggatt" in order to be able to see "Leggatt as a separate and real human being," exactly at the moment when his hat "floating on the night sea" served as saving marker with symbolic status, linking the unconscious and the real (450). More assured in his own fugitive status, the narrator also gives a definite form to the expressions of existential isolation at the outset of the novella, when the narrator, in a more meditative, less social frame of mind, contemplates his own solitude at the mouth of the river to Bangkok.[11] Finally, he assumes the heroic, decisive qualities of Leggatt by passing his self-imposed test of his own power of command, for that is what he was doing when he risked the lives of the crew to allow one man a chance to swim out into the vastness of the outer world, "Ko-Ring," and then to French Vietnam. The beginning and middle of the character's psychological development were incubation periods of the captain's self. At the end of the novella, the voices of others he had earlier spurned, like that of the first mate, take on a more sympathetic tone.

That said, the captain's social solidarity does not extend beyond his relationship with Leggatt, a fellow alumnus of Conway. The discovery of Leggatt helps the captain to own and command his transitional object, the ship and crew as stand-ins for the now vanished Leggatt, but it remains unclear the extent to which this same object is seen and shared by others in the community. The danger of this type of communication feedback loop is that everything comes from one source at the top, and outside influences in the form of warnings from nature and signs of social change are excluded, as exemplified in the captain's decision to negate the dangers presented by his nautical maneuvers. To become socially situated, the subject's transitional object, with which the subject has partially merged through his imaginative projections onto it, has undergone a form of psychological death and, paradoxically, has lived past this death into the social real, for as Winnicott writes, "destruction plays its part in making the reality, placing the object outside the self" (122). By endangering himself in taking a fugitive aboard and by endangering others in almost running the ship aground to help the same fugitive, he makes his transitional object real: he gains a stake in the actual "not me" object of the ship, as a result of his subjective involvement with the ship that has survived its figurative destruction (the intertwining of metaphorical and potentially actual). By "means of a destructive drive," his private self is thus introjected into participation within the cultural realm (125), since the captain suddenly has something personal at stake in a world of objects and thus has an incentive to make creative contributions to society. Differing from self-realization, however, cultural participation does not mean the healthy individual must become like a Romantic individualist at odds with social norms; in fact, "if the artist is searching for the self, then it can be said that in all probability that there is already some failure for that artist in the field of general creative living" (73). Rather, in health, the individual whose transitional object has undergone this psychic death and rebirth has become a conventional, active member of an evolving community and therefore feels it is enough to make incremental (non-revolutionary) contributions toward change through "the cultural pool." Conversely, Romantic artists can remain psychologically regressive, regardless of what creative genius they may bring to the world. They may dredge up psychic material for the benefit of the life energies of the community, but it does not mean they, as seekers of true-self modes of life, become a part of the community. In fact, as Girard predicts, in terms of the trope of the Romantic mad genius, like the speaker of "Kubla Khan," they remain persistently individualistic, in constant conflict with the dominant social structure of their time. This trope Conrad and other modernists also opposed.

Like a creative artist, then, through his discovery of and release from his "second self," the narrator-captain has taken one step toward freedom from excessive solipsism, but there is no reason to believe he will not immediately slip back into the state of near madness (the double binds of Girard's mimetic triangle) from which he had managed to escape through an arbitrary act of self-assertiveness in swerving the ship's course (Conrad, *Sharer* 41). Here the Conradian motif of "homo-duplex" figures as a reduced form of group solidarity rather than the quasi-supernatural doubleness of Romanticism *(CL* 3:89*)*. In *The Secret Sharer*, this is expressed as the conjoined state of a divided (signified by the secret relationship with Leggatt) and a shared experience of selfhood (that of the normal role as captain to a crew and ship) and is to some extent, therefore, a departure from a Romantic emphasis on expressive individualism. In this way, the novella as a whole depicts a move toward a version of Conrad's "homo-duplex" with the creative individual interacting within a divided "we"—rather than as heroic, Nietzschean "I"—capacity.[12] Romantic individuality interjoined with communality, or as Winnicott expresses it, an "interplay between separateness and union," must be present if a culture or an individual is to meet the threats and catastrophes of nature creatively *(Playing* 134). The resolution of Conrad's novella leaves this goal underdeveloped, even with its now seemingly self-possessed captain, who has confirmed his preference for an elitist we-mode of existence. Nevertheless, where the Nietzschean Leggatt could transcend good and evil in a response to insubordination of a crew member during a storm at sea, the narrator-captain can channel his own form of decisiveness to prevent panic among crew members during the crisis he is responsible for imposing on them. With this incomplete realization of the dialectic in mind, I turn now to Conrad's *The Shadow-Line*.

CREATIVE MIMESIS IN *THE SHADOW-LINE*

To the captain-narrator in the shadow-line, anything collective seems to represent the staid routine of the work-a-day life on a steamship, from which he wishes to escape by quitting his post as first mate on the *Melita*. He is in search of a truer, more glamorous life, as there was "no truth to be got out of" such a "prosaic waste of days" (Conrad, *Shadow-Line* 50). The unnamed captain at his first command resembles the captain in *The Secret Sharer*: he is dreamy, impulsive, and given to uncharitable and aloof attitudes toward the steward and the unemployed Hamilton residing at the Sailor's Home in Singapore. The true-self side of the psychological dialectic can be seen as the captain-narrator steps on board his new command and sees himself as "hereditary king, in a class all by [him]self" where "he was there to rule by an agency as remote from the people as inscrutable almost to [his crew] as the Grace of God" (88). He is to be the head to the body of the crew and ship, in a "pathological feedback loop" comprised of the relationship between a king and his subjects (Lawtoo, *Shadow* 100). Hence, at the outset of the voyage, while he awaits permission to sail from Bangkok, there are no communal relations between him, his crews, and the outside world; there are only traditional protocols dictating relations among crewmembers.

Starting with his unspoken rejection of a false-self bargain with nature and society,[13] *The Shadow-Line* shows how the narrator-captain changes from valuing a vertical hereditary kinship to a horizontal affective kinship based on experience, training, and the influence passed along through tradition, that is, from an "I" to a "we" type of communal belonging. But in the first hour of his new command, while gazing at himself in the mirror, he still feels as if the "composite soul, the soul of command, had whispered to [him] of long days at sea and of anxious moments" (Conrad, *Shadow-Line* 82). His mirror-gazing suggests identification with models in the nautical tradition as a tenable type of identification in terms of his ability to carry out his duties—as long as these others are not physically present or are too socially remote so as to present threats to his autonomy.

Thus, the narrator's search for a true-self mode of existence earlier in Singapore, symptomatic of a fear of dependence in Ulanov's terms, can be read in his feelings of "indifference" in his reactions to Hamilton and the steward from the Sailor's Home, and in the finality of his generalized conclusion that, since the father figure of Captain Giles, the best that humanity has to offer him, is given to a seeming fatuousness, on the whole, "human nature is not very nice" (63). In his shadow-line state as an unfulfilled sailor, without the glamour he feels is his due, he "lives atop an emptiness, a gap that [he] dreads falling into but cannot fill" (Ulanov 118). Following Girard, Ulanov notes that failing to transcend the crisis results in a masochistic or a withdrawn personality, which is what the reader sees when the narrator remains below deck and becomes, understandably, more impatient with his "bad luck," "his mistakes," and "his conscience" (Conrad, *Shadow-Line* 134). Similarly, for Winnicott, an untransformed potential space results in an indifferent disposition toward others—ultimately arising from a fear of re-experiencing the trauma of the loss of continuity with the mother.

Enabling the Winnicottian remedy for this kind of untransformed transitional space on his new command, members of the crew mediate the captain's anti-mimetic tendencies of indifference and cynicism and his need to lead others from within the ship's collective psychology rather than from without. Ransome, in trying to prevent his own heart attack while exerting himself to help others, places himself at the captain's disposal, doing just enough to adapt his actions and responses to the captain's. In addition to cooking for and attending to narrator and crew, Ransome carries on with the protocols of life at sea while allowing the captain to believe that social impulses arise within himself. The pivotal example is Ransome's standing by while the captain, at the height of his and the ship's ordeal, remains secluded below deck. Ransome says nothing until the captain suggests, "You think I should go on deck?" Ransome simply replies, "I do" (119). Together, Ransome, the chief mate Burns, as well as the cooperative crew of the ship as a whole, help the captain move toward a more horizontal affective kinship based on shared experiences instead of elite identifications.

As noted in the critical literature, Ransome and Burns may represent different sides of the narrator's psyche in a dialectical relationship with each other.[14] Ransome's presence onboard signifies beneficent goodness, while Burns's example suggests the side of the captain's personality that confronts danger in a bull-headed, irrational way by personifying nature's catastrophes as the work of evil forces. In the delirium of his fever, Burns imagines the ship held under the curse of its deceased previous captain, whom he had given a proper sea burial at the exact place where the ship stalled in a windless sea. "Skulking's no good [. . .] you can't slink past the murderous ruffian . . . You must go for him boldly . . . Show him you don't care for any of his damned tricks!" he tells the present captain after cursing the ghost of the former captain (124). Unexpectedly, he opens the captain's eyes to the reality of the crew's cultural currents by personifying impersonal natural forces as personal mythology, or delirium. As the captain observes himself, adopting and imitating Burns's talk of a vindictive, dead captain cursing the ship and its crew, he gradually opens himself to his influence by creatively interacting with others, as if they live together in a world where subjective mythology and objective fact freely intermingle. As noted by Stephen Land, both the name and the enigmatic beneficence of the faint-hearted Ransome, called upon "to give his life a ransom for many" (Matthew 20:28), justify comparisons to Christ who sacrifices his human ego for the benefit of mankind (Land 216). Ransome's example gives others the security from which to strike out into the not-me world where the subject can have a personal stake in the community. As a result of his influence, toward the end of the novella the captain appears more open to stories, superstitions, and common and ever-changing cultural mythology, even under the direst circumstances. References to *The Flying Dutchman* and Coleridge's "Ancient Mariner" align with realistic details (the dying crew, the windless ocean, the mishaps and accidents) to provide a provisional source of meaning that allows the captain to partake in the ship's cultural life, one involving Burns's visions of sinister evil and Ransome's example of beneficence. This suggests a provisional union of true-self hero and a communitarian spiritual ethos, paradoxically both separate from the ultimate source of being and united with it. As with the captain from *The Secret Sharer*, to truly experience reality as both separately indifferent and meaningfully alive, the developing individual must also experience the temporary death of the subject's projected-upon "transitional object," which in both novellas are the captains' Romantic relationships to their respective ship and crew.[15]

In terms of facilitating this experience of death in life, Ransome's defective heart as conduit to sympathy in cultural life serves as the objective corollary to Giles's admonishments about faintheartedness bookending the novella. The comment about the "nice boys" in Singapore in chapter 1 refers to a form of faintheartedness that leads one to turn away from hard work and danger, but the narrator tellingly, at that point in his development, misconstrues Giles's words to mean only effeminacy and a less heroic vision of manhood (Conrad, *Shadow-Line* 134, 55). The fainthearted Ransome is anything but a passive shirker of duty; he quietly does more work than anyone onboard at the most crucial moments during the storm, when only he, the captain and Burns comprise the crew that must manipulate the sails and steer the ship. And throughout the ship's descent into horror, Ransome appears at precisely the correct moments to impart "exactly the right tone of sympathy" (116). Due to his concern for his own literally faint heart, Ransome's influence thereby gives rise to productive dialogue—"Life was a boon to him, this precarious hard life" (132)—with Burns's panic-inducing influences on the captain during the time when it "occurs to [the narrator] that [he] had been talking somewhat in Mr. Burns' manner" (116). In this potential space between self and world, precipitated by Ransome's presence, the captain can negotiate competing psychological necessities: the need to see nature as signifying both indifference and life-giving "boon" on the one hand, and the need to confront and heed danger on the other.

Given these claims, it follows that the influence of Ransome tips the balance from a destructive influence associated with a belief in the primacy of an antimimetic true-self (like that of the deceased violin-playing captain) to one that allows for brief moments of solidarity formed in response to the common threat of Burns's spectral "enemy," the former captain and his disregard for all but himself. In a culmination of the captain-narrator's growing regard for Ransome's contribution, he remarks, "That man noticed everything, shed comfort around as he moved" (127). Through his example, heard in the narrator's account of his gradual acceptance of a mingling of voices and initiatives toward a common purpose, Ransome quells panic by not challenging anyone's projections, and thus prepares the way for a more communal identity, predicated on a relational conception of the narrator's responses to objects.[16] Prior to Burns's last defiant laughter in the face of what he imagines to be the former captain's curse, Ransome's quietness had offered a human equivalent to the death-mimicking silence that had previously threatened to dissolve Burns's sense of self, and to some extent the narrator's too, into mimetic "indifferentiation" or continuity with the stillness of the sea, when the predominant mood on board was helplessness in the face of the enemy.[17] Appearing at important points in the novella, the word "enemy" refers to the various influences signifying the reality of death, from the curse of the former captain to the disease afflicting almost every member of the crew, to the windless sea that takes on an increasingly anthropomorphized sinister and even ghostly aspect. After acknowledging Ransome's example of a disposition toward a necessary acceptance of the world, the captain and crew can make creative use of Burns's projections in order to endure the destructive element. Certainly, the deceased former captain of the ship could have navigated such a predicament without listening to Burns or Ransome, but the novella as a whole, with its dedication "To Borys and the others who like himself have crossed in early youth the shadow-line of their generation with love," warns that a new generation facing a world at war with itself must cross the "grand miroir / De mon desepoir" in a new way, together in a spirit of love and sacrifice (47).

CONRAD'S NOVELLA AS TRANSITIONAL OBJECT

The novellas discussed may be read as part of a long-running dialectic between individualism and communalism, self and world, resulting in a limited "I" type of solidarity with the outside world in the *The Secret Sharer*, and a transient, hard-won "We" type in *The Shadow-Line*. Similar to a transformed transitional object, random sensory details and voices become fleeting, socially recognizable forms under the nurturing influences of a novel that performs that part of the human subject that "mothers" rather than foists itself onto others in the form of the straightforward philosophical or scientific truths which are contrasted with "artistic truth" in the Preface to *"Narcissus"* (Conrad, "Preface" 139). A type of mimetic relationship found in a passage from Conrad's Preface depicts the sharing of, rather than competition for, being in the metaphor of a reader as a busy person from the work-a-day world who takes a break to observe a distant laborer at work:

> Sometimes, stretched at ease in the shade of a roadside tree, we watch the motions of a labourer in a distant field, and after a time, begin to wonder

languidly as to what the fellow may be at. If we know he is trying to lift a stone, to dig a ditch, to uproot a stump, we look with a more real interest at his efforts; we are disposed to condone the jar of his agitation upon the restfulness of the landscape: and even in a brotherly frame of mind, we may bring ourselves to forgive his failure. We understood his object, and, after all, the fellow has tried, and perhaps he had not the strength, and perhaps he had not the knowledge. We forgive, go on our way—and forget. (142)

The moments of reverie watching a character at work seen as a metaphor for reading a novel or encountering art resembles an adult form of transitional space for experiencing the presence of the other through a kind of negative capability without a prescriptive cultural agenda. In Conrad's Preface, a novel, instead of a church or a person, opens one to a sufficient cause of desire by presenting itself as "all the truth of life accepted for a moment, as a moment of vision" without announcing itself as such, in a response of life to the "eternal rest" suggested in the "restfulness of the landscape" (142).

Conrad's "solidarity in mysterious origin, in toil, in joy, in hope, in uncertain fate, which binds men to each other and all mankind to the visible world" may therefore be glimpsed in disparate, fleeting sensations of "truth," as opposed to a bird's-eye view of it (141). This touches on Ian Watt's question put to Conrad's Preface of how the reader is to go "if not from the Many to the One, at least from the irreducible pluralism of the visible world to 'the very truth of their existence'" (80). One answer to this question, centered as it is on Conrad's vexed and inconsistent portrayal of human "solidarity," is that this truth mentioned in the Preface may be that found defined elsewhere in Conrad as a "spectral illumination," one that, according to Alvin Alpert, does not go to the very truth of existence, but rather only insofar as the "minor insights and partial enlightenments" of every person's lived experience meet the historical, social, and physical objectivity of that same experience (Alpert 41).[18] In other words, the impossibility of the attainment of absolute forms of enlightenment (knowledge of the infinite, etc.) leading to a perfect social solidarity may instead prompt the seeker to suffice themselves with a diffused sense of truth found in those moments when objects in reality are seen momentarily to exist in their own right, separate from the perceiver, and only hint at a more transpersonal source of knowledge. The narrator of *The Secret Sharer* gains a stake in the separate reality of his ship through a process of letting his personal investment in it broaden to illuminate the prospects of the existence of a reality just beyond that investment. In *The Shadow-Line*, the narrator goes into seclusion below deck where in the presence of Ransome he is induced to give up hope of absolute control and take part in the struggles of others to gain a collective stake in "this precarious hard life," where creative participation rather than the insights of creative genius is called for. So construed, both situations find resonance in Conrad's aesthetic ideas wherein facts imitate truth: the "commonplace surface of words" against the responsive nurturance of "magic suggestiveness" (Preface 140). From this perspective, Conrad's "mysterious sources" (141) for truth may turn out to be found in his readers' world-creating transitional object, one marking the difference and interplay between the self that is a "self only in relation to certain interlocutors" and the "punctual self as pure independent consciousness" (Taylor 172).

This work was supported by The Catholic University of Korea, 2019.

NOTES

1. Regarding this idea Reineke writes, "Winnicott, as interpreted by Ulanov, delineates acquisitive mimesis and a violent sacred as well as creative mimesis and a nonviolent sacred" (83).

2. Winnicott consistently credits Melanie Klein for laying the groundwork for his work on transitional objects, and object relations in general, *Playing and Reality* (12–13). Klein and Winnicott emphasize the role of the maternal element, where it is not only the Oedipal complex that is important but the mother's or the parents' capacity to "hold" the child to help them develop a strong sense of self. Another modernist, Virginia Woolf, met Klein and had a favorable impression of her theory of seeing the mother as the source of creativity and life (Roe and Sellers 265).

3. In contrast to the self as web, Charles Taylor, a fellow traveler with Girard, thinks of "the punctual self [. . .] as pure independent consciousness," to be a mistaken form of primary creativity from a "romantic" novel's point of view (172). Girard claims "the term romantic for the works which reflect the presence of a mediator without ever revealing it and the term novelistic for the works which reveal this presence" (*Desire* 15). A focus on "interindividuality" or intersubjectivity lays the foundation for all Girard's literary interpretation (*Theater* 67). For Girard, novelistic literature reveals the presence of acquisitive mimesis in which a disciple copies the desire of his model who is his mediator for the desire for an object.

4. This recapitulation of the scapegoat mechanism in culture is taken from Girard's *Violence and the Sacred* (171).

5. Cultural experience is located here in the sense that creative play originates in potential or transitional spaces, "where the coexistence of continuity and contiguity, or the joining together of union and separation, happen in a trust-inducing manner. They happen in a transition space where "continuity is giving place to contiguity" (*PR* 136).

6. Lawtoo makes this reversal of a tit-for-tat cycle of relationships built on violence particularly clear in his analysis of Conrad's "The Duel" where the story inverts the compulsive cycle of violence between combatants in its mirror representation of their battle maneuvers in order to reverse the constant of state of mimesis in their violent gestures and arrive at a rapprochement (*Conrad's Shadow* 22).

7. Ulanov sees the false self as a "condition of schizoid splitting that aggravates rather than heals" but that in health "it functions to protect the true self [. . .] through normal social politeness [and] the severe hiding and sealing up of the germ of one's uniqueness in order to defend against exploitation and annihilation" (48).

8. The ensuing transference of subjective experience, which is emblematic of the story as a whole, justifies psychological interpretation, according to Douglas Kerr, starting with Guerard's seminal critical forward to *The Secret Sharer*. Such interpretations have taken their cues from two tropes, one of which is "delayed decoding, [. . .] disorienting moments in a narrative where a subjective impression is narrated, but its cause or meaning is withheld for a while. Both devices foreground the subjectivity of literary representation" (49).

9. For example, Daphna Erdinast-Vulcan sees the narrator's creation of his double in Leggatt as born out of a need to "objectify" and create a "bogus" version of himself in order to suppress his sense of responsibility to own up to his ethical "obligation that comes with the position of command" (455–56). Brian Richardson points out how "strange," "irresponsible," and "irrational" the narrator is (461–62).

10. In the case of an infant, this allowance is the pivotal, initial moment of the creation of illusion, in which this nurturing presence is the mother's breast that the infant believes is an extension of his body. Later, this vague illusion takes a shape or form in the infant's mind, which is the transitional object that is the precedent for the creation of other symbolic objects such as the corner of a blanket or a toy (Winnicott, *Playing* 16–17).

11. Showing a firmer conviction in the inviolability of his solitude than at the outset, he exclaims, "Nothing! No one in the world should stand now between us, throwing a shadow on the way of perfect knowledge and mute affection, the perfect communion of a seaman with his first command" (Conrad, *Sharer* 42).

12. While he doesn't mention Winnicott as the key to understanding Conradian solidarity arising through creative mimesis, Lawtoo sees "Conrad's lifelong fascination with homo duplex as affective mimesis, a form of a form of behavioral imitation whose primary characteristic consists in generating a psychological confusion between self and other(s) which, in turn, deprives subjects of their full rational presence to selfhood, of their capacity to think rationally, of their individual substance, as it were" ("Horror of Mimesis" 46).

13. Conrad's *Under Western Eyes* (1911) develops the concept of the Western "bargain with fate"—its judicial and economic systems in a superimposed relation to its history and land—as a contrast to the impracticality of a more spiritually and socially authentic one (95). This contrast appears to be another dialectic in Conrad's novels, which I here liken to that between the world and true self, with the straightjacketed Westerner living a true self reaction to the fear of the loss of being presented by the vastness of the Russian landscape. It also suggests a Conradian example of the modernist tendency toward the mimetic pull of a participation mystique, wherein less self-conscious individuals, like "the children of the sea" of "*Narcissus*," or the Russian folk of *Under Western Eyes*, are believed to live in greater proximity to a primal reality.

14. Stephen K. Land's *Conrad and the Paradox of Plot* argues that Ransome's faintheartedness is something the captain must overcome and squelch and is not responsible for precipitating the captain's social solidarity, unlike my position here.

15. Winnicott explains the phenomenon as follows: "[H]e will find that after 'subject relates to object' comes 'subject destroys object' (as it becomes external); and then may come

'*object survives* destruction by the subject,' but there may or may not be survival. A new feature thus arrives in the theory of object-relating. The subject says to the object: 'I destroyed you,' and the object is there to receive the communication. From now on the subject says: 'Hullo object!' 'I destroyed you.' 'I love you.' 'You have value for me because of your survival of my destruction of you.' [. . .] In other words, because of the survival of the object, the subject may now have started to live a life in the world of objects, and so the subject stands to gain immeasurably; but the price has to be paid in acceptance of the ongoing destruction in unconscious fantasy relative to object-relating" (*Playing* 120).

16. The mimetic theorist and physicist Pablo Bandera sums it up as follows: "A cheap romance novel may present desire as a sort of magnetic attraction toward some object of lust or greed [. . .]. More intelligent novels trace out the subtle and complex elements within a network of relationships that define the dynamics of desire" (57).

17. See Lawtoo's discussion of the "two oppositional tendencies [in Conrad]: one toward life and antimimetic differentiation, the other toward death and mimetic indifferentiation" (*Shadow* 233).

18. Alvin Alpert argues that what Marlow's frame narrator refers to as "spectral illuminations" in *Heart of Darkness* can be "understood to refer to the kind of insights into the world we have after we stop looking for perfect knowledge" (42). Alpert claims the alternative is to be "part of the liberal ideal of enlightenment, whose famous mission was to 'civilize the savages'" (42).

WORKS CITED

Alpert, Alvin. *Partial Enlightenments: What Modern Literature and Buddhism Can Teach Us about Living Well Without Perfection.* Columbia University Press, 2021.

Bandera, Pablo. *Reflection in the Waves: The Interindividual Observer in a Quantum Mechanical World.* Michigan State University Press, 2019.

Conrad, Joseph. *The Collected Letters of Joseph Conrad.* 9 vols., edited by Laurence Davies, et al., Cambridge University Press, 1983–2008.

———. "Preface to *The Nigger of the 'Narcissus.'*" 1914, *The Secret Sharer and Other Stories*, edited by John G. Peters, W.W. Norton, 2015, pp. 139–42.

———. *The Secret Sharer.* 1910, *The Secret Sharer and Other Stories*, edited by John G. Peters, W.W. Norton, 2015, pp. 7–42.

———. *The Shadow-Line.* 1917, *The Secret Sharer and Other Stories*, edited by John G. Peters, W.W. Norton, 2015, pp. 47–148.

———. *Typhoon.* 1902, *The Secret Sharer and Other Stories*, edited by John G. Peters, W.W. Norton, 2015, pp. 259–325.

Erdinast-Vulcan, Daphna. "The Seductions of the Aesthetic: 'The Secret Sharer.'" *The Secret Sharer and Other Stories*, edited by John G. Peters, W.W. Norton, 2015, pp. 451–58.

Freud, Sigmund. *The Interpretation of Dreams.* Translated by James Strachey, Avon, 1965.

Girard, Rene. *Deceit, Desire, and the Novel.* Translated by Yvonee Freccero, The Johns Hopkins University Press, 1966.

———. *A Theater of Envy.* St. Augustine's Press, 2004.

———. *Things Hidden Since the Foundation of the World.* Translated by Stephen Bann and Michael Metterer, Stanford University Press, 1987.

---. *Violence and the Sacred*. Translated by Patrick Gregory, The Johns University Press, 1977.
Guerard, Alfred J. "The Secret Sharer and the Other Self." *The Secret Sharer and Other Stories*, edited by John G. Peters, W.W. Norton, 2015, pp. 447–51.
Jasanoff, Maya. *The Dawn Watch: Joseph Conrad in a Global World*. Penguin, 2017.
Kerr, Douglas. 2015. "Approaching Conrad Through Theory." *The New Cambridge Companion to Joseph Conrad*, edited by J.H. Stape, Cambridge University Press, 2014, pp. 44–57.
Klein, Melanie. "A Contribution to the Psychogenesis of Manic-Depressive States." *Essential Papers on Object Relations*, edited by Peter Buckley, New York University Press, 1986, pp. 42–70.
Land, Stephen K. *Conrad and the Paradox of Plot*. Macmillan, 1984.
Larabee, Mark D. "'A Mysterious System': Topographical Fidelity and the Charting of Imperialism in Joseph Conrad's Siamese Waters." *The Secret Sharer and Other Stories*, edited by John G. Peters, W.W. Norton, 2015, pp. 480–98.
Lawtoo, Nidesh. *Conrad's Shadow: Catastrophe, Mimesis, Theory*. Michigan State University Press, 2016.
---. "The Horror of Mimesis." *Conradiana*, vol. 42, nos.1–2, 2010, pp. 45–72.
---. *The Phantom of the Ego: Modernism and the Mimetic Unconscious*. Michigan State University Press, 2013.
Peters, John G. "Preface." *The Secret Sharer and Other Stories*, edited by John G. Peters, W.W. Norton, 2015, pp. ix–xii.
Reineke, Martha J. "Transforming Space: Creativity, Destruction, and Mimesis in Winnicott and Girard." *Contagion: Journal of Violence, Mimesis, and Culture*, vol. 14, 2007, pp. 79–95.
Renner, Stanley W. "The Secret Sharer, Nietzsche, and Conrad's New Man." *Conradiana*, vol. 44, nos. 2–3, 2012, pp. 145–61.
Richardson, Brian. "Constructing Conrad's 'The Secret Sharer': Suppressed Narratives, Subaltern Reception, and the Act of Interpretation." *The Secret Sharer and Other Stories*, edited by John G. Peters, W.W. Norton, 2015, pp. 458–69.
Rising, Catharine. "*Typhoon*: Conrad's Tacit Recessional." *Conradiana*, vol. 35, nos. 1–2, 2003, pp. 123–32.
Roe, Sue, and Susan Sellers, eds. *The Cambridge Companion to Virginia Woolf*. Cambridge University Press, 2000.
Taylor, Charles. *Sources of the Self: The Making of Modern Identity*. Harvard University Press, 1989.
Ulanov, Ann Bedford. *Finding Space: Winnicott, God, and Psychic Reality*. Westminster John Knox Press, 2001.
Watt, Ian. *Conrad in the Nineteenth Century*. University of California Press, 1979.
Winnicott, D. W. "Communicating and Not Communicating Leading to a Study of Certain Opposites." *The Maturational Processes and the Facilitating Environment: Studies in the Theory of Emotional Development*, Hogarth, 1965, pp. 179–92.
---. "Ego Distortion in Terms of True and False Self." *The Maturational Processes and the Facilitating Environment: Studies in the Theory of Emotional Development*, Hogarth, 1965, pp.140–52.
---. *Playing and Reality*. Routledge, 2005.

Review

Reading *Reading Conrad*.
A Review of J. Hillis Miller's *Reading Conrad*.
Edited by John G. Peters and Jakob Lothe.
Columbus: The Ohio State University Press, 2017. pp. 260.
ISBN: 9780814254356.

As its two-word title elegantly suggests, J. Hillis Miller's *Reading Conrad* has a double focus that reflects the twofold purpose of the collection. On the one hand, this volume, carefully edited by two distinguished Conrad scholars, John G. Peters and Jakob Lothe, assembles the entirety of the articles and chapters Miller wrote on Joseph Conrad during his prolific career as one of the most influential literary critics and theorists of the twentieth- and twenty-first centuries. Including texts written from the 1960s to the 2010s, the volume makes available illuminating, widely influential, yet not always easily traceable essays that had so far been disseminated in different books and collections, had often been anthologized, and yet, somewhat surprisingly given the depth, scope, and critical intensity of Miller's careerlong engagement with Conrad, had never been assembled in a single volume before. As Peters and Lothe state in the foreword: "Perhaps it is the fact that Miller has been a leading figure within different trends of literary theory, especially (but not only) deconstruction, that has allowed us to overlook the significance of his contribution to Conrad studies" (xv). *Reading Conrad* fills a significant gap in Conrad studies, new modernist studies, and literary theory and criticism more generally. Published in the "Theory and Interpretation of Narrative Series" at Ohio State University Press, it is a great fortune that the entirety of Miller's seminal, penetrating, and deservedly canonical essays on Conrad are now finally available for new generations of students, teachers, and researchers to read and reread.

The question of reading leads us to the second word in the title, which adds a doubling, performative effect to the volume. *Reading Conrad*, in fact, is not only of interest for *what* it says about Conrad's influential narratives, but also, and equally important, for *how* it performs an art that is speedily disappearing in an increasingly digitized age but is absolutely vital for literary studies and the humanities as a whole: namely, the art of "reading," understood "in the strong sense, [as] an active responsible response that renders justice to a book by generating more language in its turn" (88). While Miller is indebted to what the New Critics called "close reading" and phenomenologists "hermeneutics," he prefers to designate this performative art as "rhetorical reading." Miller's interest in rhetoric is not primarily understood as an art of persuasion but as a critical attention to reading linguistic tropes that do not rest on a unitary and organic conception of the work of art (New Criticism); nor is its strength guaranteed by the "reference to the words to something distinct from them" (130), say, a theoretical code of interpretation, or the referential world the text represents and thus simply imitates (hermeneutics).[1] Instead, rhetorical reading pays considerable formal attention to the "words themselves in their interplay" (130), including a special focus on shifts of perspective, narrative frames, linguistic tensions and contradictions, figurative language, etymologies and, last but not least, irony—all of which, Miller convincingly demonstrates, are central to reading literature in general and to reading Conrad in particular.

Reading Conrad, then, is an untimely Janus-faced book: it is as much a lesson on reading *Conrad* as on the importance of *reading* tout court. If "reading as an *art*"—to borrow a phrase from another master of the art of reading, or philologist, who looms larger that is often realized in Miller's interpretations—has been "thoroughly unlearned" (Nietzsche 10),[2] *Reading Conrad* encourages new generations of readers immersed in increasingly fast digital media to slow down a bit and learn the pleasure of this art again via the medium of Conrad's exemplary narratives.

The volume starts with a Foreword in which Lothe and Peters carefully trace the shifts of theoretical emphasis at play in Miller's readings of Conrad over half a century. They do so by competently situating them in the larger context of Miller's career-long engagement with literary theory—from his early alignment with phenomenology, to deconstruction, to his most recent ethical turn. It is followed by a brief Introduction written specifically for this volume titled "Conrad and Me" in which Miller recalls, in a confessional mood, his first experience of reading Conrad as he found *Typhoon* on his father's bookshelf—a telling tale, or rather, parable, that frames the whole book and to which I promise to return.

The bulk of the volume is composed of seven chapters that trace the historical development of Miller's writings on Conrad, from the seminal chapters included in one of his first books, *Poets of Reality* (1965), to the present. Schematically put, they include: a phenomenologically-oriented analysis of the meaning of "darkness" in *The Secret Agent* and *Heart of Darkness* (chapter 1); a deconstructive reading of narrative repetitions in *Lord Jim* that marks Miller's break with New Criticism (chapter 2); his rhetorical reading of *Heart of Darkness* as a "parable" of an apocalypse that is never now, which is situated at the center of the volume and is still one of the most influential essays in Conrad studies (chapter 3). This central chapter is then followed by two other readings of Conrad's most famous tale in which Miller responds to two major critical/ theoretical interventions in Conrad studies: the first, "Joseph Conrad: Should we Read *Heart of Darkness*?" offers an implicit reply to postcolonial critic and author Chinua Achebe, who in "An Image of Africa," (in)famously questioned the legitimacy of teaching *Heart of Darkness* (chapter 4); the second, "Revisiting *Heart of Darkness* Revisited" is Miller's explicit theoretical engagement with Philippe Lacoue-Labarthe's "The Horror of the West," an essay he considered an "event" for Conrad studies and led Miller to "revisit" his reading of Conrad's most famous tale "in the company" of the French philosopher who shared Miller's friendship with Jacques Derrida (chapter 5). Lastly, the volume includes Miller's most recent engagements with ethics in his reading of "The Secret Sharer" (chapter 6) and concludes with a detailed analysis of the role (the absence of) community plays in *Nostromo* (chapter 7).

Originally included in influential books like *Poets of Reality* (1965), *Fiction and Repetition* (1982), *Communities in Fiction* (2015), among other collections of essays that mark different stages in Miller's intellectual development, the attentive reader will soon notice that, while not forming a unified whole, the volume is more than the sum of its individual chapters. There is, in fact, a spiraling interplay between reading and theory at play in *Reading Conrad* that serves as an Ariadne's thread secretly connecting these heterogeneous essays and generating rhetorical twists and turns in Miller's impressively diverse readings of Conrad that are as critical as theoretical. As Lothe and Peters state in the Foreword, "although Miller's analyses are informed by theory" (xvi) and offer admirable performances of some of the major theoretical schools of the twentieth century (most notably, phenomenology, New Criticism, deconstruction, narrative theory, stretching to include his recent philosophical concerns with ethics and community), "the theories are informed—modified, refined, and sometimes challenged—by his analyses and close readings" (xvi). In this double literary and theoretical sense, Conrad's fictions turn out to be not only one of the constant reference points on which Miller's provisionally anchored his shifting critical perspectives; they also play an exemplary role in the emergence of some of the most influential theoretical turns that have formed and continue to transform the destiny of literary studies over the past fifty years— from the linguistic turn to the ethical turn, the affective turn to the mimetic turn or re-turn.

The reader who worries that Miller's theoretical analyses of Conrad remain simply confined within the sphere of high theory, or within the boundaries of "the text," without paying attention to realities *hors-texte* that affect real, embodied people in a referential, material world, has no reasons to worry. The book has, once again, a double-orientation. It is true that in contrapuntal relation to dominant trends in cultural studies that privilege historical and political contexts over the words in the text, Miller, despite his shifts of perspective, consistently pays close rhetorical attention to Conrad's literary language, unveiling the different layers of meanings of his tales intrinsically—that is, from the *inside*-out. But it is equally true that, for Miller, the distinction between inside and outside is far from stable and watertight. Hence, he also uses his illuminating insights into Conrad's take on responsibility, imperialist exploitation, ethical solidarity, and community to cast light on the exterior world, a world in fast transformation which, in a spiraling feedback loop, redirects readers' critical gaze to new aspects of the tales—from the *outside*-in. There is no contradiction at play in this spiraling approach but a methodological principle Lothe and Peters describe as follows: "Miller reacts not just to critical theories in literary studies, but also to what he observes in his contemporary world. His criticism is thus informed both by theory and, broadly understood, politics—and his politics has a distinctly ethical component" (xv). This is a crucial point in Miller's understanding of reading more generally. He repeatedly confirms it elsewhere, as he states, for instance: "Since 'reading' in this sense is indispensable to any responsible concern for the relations of literature to what is outside, it would be a catastrophe for the study of literature if the insights of deconstruction, along with those of the New Criticism [...] were to be forgotten ... in some imagined historical 'development'" ("Function" 263).

Miller's commitment to articulating an interplay between words inside the text and the world outside has often gone unnoticed by readers who hastily confined him to second-hand understandings of "deconstruction" (a term, which, by the way, Miller no longer uses precisely for the misunderstandings it continues to generate); yet it is absolutely crucial for grasping the forward-looking dimension of his readings. Speaking of Miller's first essays on Conrad, Lothe and Peters observe: "Rereading those chapters on Conrad we have been struck by just how far ahead of his time Miller was" (viii). This forward-looking tendency, I would like to argue, applies, in strikingly different ways, to all the chapters that compose the volume—a performative effect of the method of slow reading Miller advocates.

Since an accurate and informed overview of the volume can be found in the Foreword to this volume, I will refrain from providing a summary of each chapter, if only because that would not be reading in Miller's sense but simply a phantom of reading. Nor am I particularly interested in conforming to the standard expectations of offering a severe evaluation of the limits of the book under review, and for a double reason: first, because strong readings are increasingly rare and ought to be celebrated in an age in which, as Miller lucidly recognizes, "The era of printed literature is now coming to an end, in what promises to be a long, drawn-out-agony, as new media replace the printed book" (182); and second, because such hypercritical attempts tend to set up an unflattering mirror that reveals more about the mimetic rivalries, jealousies, and resentments that plague an increasingly competitive and receding field than about the book under evaluation.

Instead, let me try something different. Since, for Miller, "Reading is an active, transformative interpretation, not a passive reception" (136–7), I would like to take some first, tentative steps in the direction of reading *Reading Conrad*. This is not all that easy given the density of the artist that hosts the reader, which is itself redoubled by the sophistication of the "critic as host." And yet, it is worth attempting in order to foreground the untimely nature of Miller's critical and theoretical approach and outline the importance of this book for Conrad studies, literary studies, and for reading tout court. I shall thus focus on both sides of this Janus-faced title, and, in the process, attempt to open up some lines of inquiry for future readers of Conrad who will certainly find a powerful source of critical and theoretical inspiration in *Reading Conrad*.

Chapter 1, titled "The Darkness and *The Secret Agent*," is double-faced. It is as much a critical reading of the meaning of "darkness" that traverses many of Conrad's tales via the case studies of *Heart of Darkness* and *The Secret Agent* as it is a theoretical account of the metaphysical foundations, which, for Miller, go to the heart of Conrad's "nihilism," and of his attempt to go beyond it. On the side of criticism, Miller relies on methods he inherited from New Criticism as well as from phenomenology, most notably from the Belgian-born critic, Georges Poulet, who was his colleague early in his career at Johns Hopkins. Thus, he pays close attention to multiple "narrators and points of view," "reconstruction of the chronological sequence," the "use of the framing story" (13), all of which Conrad uses to generate what Miller describes as a form of phenomenological suspension through which "the world is put in parentheses, seen as a pure phenomenon" (14). Conrad, and at one remove, Miller, both use phenomenological lenses to first bracket and then unmask a "concern for the world-wide expansion of Western man's will to power" (6). It is worth noting that this method is not without forward-reaching insights. In fact, the expansion of human, all-too-human, will to power has continued to increase exponentially since Miller wrote these untimely lines and remains more relevant than ever in the age of the Anthropocene and the sixth mass extinction he discusses at the twilight of his career (see Cohen, Colebrook, and Miller, eds.).

And yet, it is indicative of Miller's relation to theory that while a method of reading provides the starting point for the literary analyses, reading Conrad, in turn, leads Miller to reframe the method in order to account for words on the page that do not fit neatly within the initial phenomenological frame. His analysis of "darkness" is significant in this respect. In fact, for Miller, the darkness that underscores Conrad's nihilism is not simply a literary trope to interpret, or a phenomenon to observe impartially; nor can it be only understood in terms of a moral, cultural, political, or psychological reality that exists as a theoretical construct independent of the text—though it can be both. Thus, if Miller recognizes that darkness, for Conrad, entails the "effacement of the ego" (7), he specifies that "it would be an error to identify it with the Freudian unconscious" (21). Clearly, already at this early stage in his career, Miller is not applying any theory from the outside-in. Instead, he illuminates a crucial aspect of Conrad's account of darkness from the inside-out. This intrinsic perspective, in turn, puts him in a position to shed light on a fundamental aspect of Conrad's poetics that, to this day, tends to be overlooked. Miller, in fact, dares the unfashionable observation that darkness for Conrad "is a metaphysical entity" (21). Whether the focus is on *Heart of Darkness, The Shadow-Line*, or the text to which he devotes most attention in this chapter, *The Secret Agent*, in Miller's reading "the darkness is not nothingness, and it is not limited to the depth of human nature. It is the basic stuff of the universe, the uninterrupted. It is what remains, horrifyingly, when every thing or color has disappeared" (22).

While Miller's metaphysical take on darkness paved the way for further analyses of Conrad in the last decades of the twentieth century, most notably, Royal Roussel's *The Metaphysics of Darkness* (1971), it also anticipates a more recent metaphysical turn in Conrad studies. To gauge its foundations, it is worth recalling the aesthetic and ontological principles on which Conrad's metaphysics fundamentally rests. Since the author under consideration is an artist, it is perhaps not surprising that Miller detects an artistic metaphysics that rests on two related, yet contrasting, mimetic principles at play in Conrad: one luminous and clear, the other dark and chthonic. As he puts it, "the heart of darkness exists beneath Apollonian clarity, ready to burst out and change the most civilized man into a savage" (22). Clarity versus darkness, rationality versus irrationality, civilization versus savagery, or, as Nietzsche, whose philosophical categories Miller borrows in this chapter—from "nihilism" to "will to power," "the eternal return" to the "Apollonian"—would put it: Apollonian mimesis based on the deceiving laws of representation (dreams) versus

Dionysian mimesis based on true ecstatic impersonations (clamor). This, the attentive reader will see for herself, is arguably the artistic metaphysics that gives birth to Miller's reading Conrad.[3]

Now, I find it revealing of the strength of Miller's reading method that the metaphysical dimension of Conrad's take on darkness, which was marginalized in the last decades of the twentieth century, has recently returned to inform a philosophical turn in Conrad studies in the twenty-first century. Theoretically-inclined readers will, in fact, find in an essay Miller calls "one of the best [essays] ever written" (157) on *Heart of Darkness*—namely, Philippe Lacoue-Labarthe's "The Horror of the West," as well as in the philosophical echoes this essay generated, including Miller's response in chapter 7, "Revisiting '*Heart of Darkness* Revisited'"—a starting point to reevaluate Conrad's metaphysics of darkness precisely along the distinction between Apollonian and Dionysian mimesis Miller had foreseen as early as in 1965. Moreover, the reader who returns to these chapters from the perspective of a new philosophical turn in Conrad studies will notice that despite, or better, because of Miller's attention to language, he uncovers a Conradian metaphysics that blurs the ontological distinction between nature and human nature, matter and spirit, words inside the text and matters outside the text, along lines that anticipate new reevaluations of the materiality, precariousness, and fragility of human life in an age in which the nature/culture binary no longer holds. As Miller puts it: "Man in one way participates in the majesty of matter that never dies. Though his body is organic rather than inorganic, it comes from matter and returns to it" (40). Could it be, then, that Miller, on the shoulders of Conrad's artistic metaphysics, is, in such moments, beginning to trace a human/non-human conjunctive-disjunction in which "Man is the meeting place of matter and spirit, and is riven apart by their contradiction" (47)? That is, a meeting place that crosses the nature/culture binary along non-anthropocentric lines we are only beginning to unearth during a new genealogical epoch that is now known as the Anthropocene? A question for ecologically-inclined readers to pursue.

Chapter 2, titled "*Lord Jim*: Repetition as Subversion of Organic Form," is one of the most influential essays in the collection. Its significance is thus as critical as it is theoretical, for it is a watershed piece that marks Miller's transition from phenomenology and New Criticism to deconstruction. There are a number of linguistic traces that mark this transition. From Miller's critique of aesthetic notions of "organic unity" based on a mimesis of an action with a beginning, middle and end (Aristotle), to his decentering of theological/Romantic principles that define the poem as centered on the "Image of God" (Coleridge), to his injunction to the critic to "enter the text, follow its threads as they weave in and out" (58), this essay outlines a destabilizing conception of truth understood in terms of "appearing and disappearing" (58) that bears the traces of Jacques Derrida's deconstruction of Western metaphysics of presence. Derrida, whose deconstruction sits on the shoulders of Heidegger, provides the starting point—or better, *coup d'envoi*—for Miller's subsequent deconstructive steps. Miller's reading of *Lord Jim*, with its "echoing episodes" (68) woven together in a "pattern of similarity and difference" (69) whose "chain of repetitions" (67) generate narrative indeterminacies and temporal complexities the critic can endlessly trace and retrace, is an admirable illustration of the twists and turns a deconstructive reading can take. It also remains one of the best critical case studies to introduce deconstruction in a class of literary theory today.

And yet, the reader will also notice that Miller does not simply "apply" Derrida's method in this chapter. Quite the contrary, he finds his starting point in another French philosopher who is often opposed to deconstruction these days but that genealogical lenses reveal to support a similar (Nietzschean) metaphysics central to *Reading Conrad*. Gilles Deleuze's account of repetition and difference in *Logique du Sens*, which Miller quotes in the introduction that precedes his reading of *Lord Jim* in *Fiction and Repetition*, finds, once again, in Nietzsche's double take on mimesis, if not a stable and unitary origin, at least its starting point—or better, its *Stoßpunkt*. What are we to make of this second, less visible repetition in which mimesis, in its double manifestation of copy and simulacrum, continues to play a role? As Miller explains, Deleuze, on the shoulders of Nietzsche, who in turn finds himself in an agonistic dialogue with Plato, sets up "two alternative theories of repetition" (*Fiction* 5). In the first, Platonic model "the validity of the mimetic copy is established by its truth of correspondence to what it copies" (16). That is, an ideal model or origin that promotes an ontology of sameness based on the logic of "resemblance" (Deleuze 297). In the second, Nietzschean/Deleuzian model, we have a world based on "difference" which does not generate copies but, rather, what Deleuze calls "simulacrum" and Nietzsche calls "phantom." This is a mimetic repetition without a singular origin or model that gives only an "impression of resemblance [*impression de resemblance*]" but that introduces a world of "becoming [*devenir*]" (298) instead—what Deleuze, echoing Nietzsche, also calls a "Dionysiac machine [*machine dionysiaque*]" (303). Many readers have identified the Derridean origins of Miller's claim that the "reader is not permitted to go outside the text" (*Reading* 72) in order to find a "center" or "origin" that would stabilize the play of (narrative, temporal, and linguistic) repetitions that constitute *Lord Jim*. And yet, simply paying attention to the words on the page also reveals a different, less-known, yet parallel and supplementary story. In fact, Miller's deeper genealogical foundations rest on two competing theories of mimesis which he traces, via Deleuze and Nietzsche, all the way back to Plato. They reveal an interplay between mimetic simulations and linguistic traces that have, to my knowledge, largely been left in the background so far and deserve to be brought into the foreground in the twenty-first century.

This genealogical insight that traces—via Derrida and Deleuze—the ontology at play in Miller's reading of Conrad back to Nietzsche has both critical and theoretical implications that lead me to nuance a key principle of deconstruction. Despite its explicit anti-mimetic stance which in-*forms* (gives form to) Miller's rhetorical readings, his fundamental position on mimesis seems, in fact, to be at least double. Like the moon, mimesis has two sides: one visible, luminous and Apollonian, the other invisible, dark and Dionysian, and both mimetic sides might be secretly at play in Reading Conrad. Let us take a closer look.

On the visible side, Miller consistently aligns deconstruction *contra* a straightforwardly mimetic or realistic conception of literature which grounds the validity of a reading in external referents in a "pseudo-historical or mimetic way" (109). This is the well-known, anti-mimetic/realistic stance Miller develops, *with* Derrida, *contra* Plato and the hierarchical metaphysics it entails. According to Plato, in fact, the work of art is "twice removed" (Miller 60) from the world of ideal forms it is a copy or mimesis of. In a doubling move, this is also the anti-mimetic stance Miller develops contra Lacoue-Labarthe. Thus, he says, for instance, that "Lacoue-Labarthe [. . .] stresses narrative complexities in his reading, and as for Plato, these complexities of mimesis are grounded in a realist or referential diegesis" (163). Deconstruction is indeed radically opposed to a straightforwardly realistic conception of literature understood in terms of a representation of reality based on a simple imitation or mimesis of external referents. Hence Miller repeatedly stresses his opposition to "mimetic theories of art" (59) that go from Plato to Coleridge and reduce the poem to "an image of an image" (59), mere phantoms of shadows "twice removed" (60) from the transcendental world of ideal Forms. Miller, like Derrida and Deleuze before him, is clearly Nietzschean in his anti-Platonic suspicion of mimesis as debased reflection of a more ideal light.

On the other, less-visible, darker side, both Lacoue-Labarthe and Conrad, read in the company of that double-faced philosopher par excellence who is Nietzsche, might also help us supplement this anti-mimetic approach by foregrounding a second, more protean, and destabilizing conception of mimesis that, I believe, remains at play in deconstruction in general and in Miller's rhetorical reading of Conrad in particular. I hasten to add that my aim here is not to deconstruct an opposition that, as Miller is the first to know, was never stable in the first place. Rather, my goal is to look ahead to a mimetic turn— or *re*-turn of mimesis—that is currently returning to the foreground of the theoretical scene, started in new modernist studies, is fully at play in Conrad studies, and was already indirectly reflected in Miller's careful reading of Conrad. To borrow a conceptual polarity Miller introduces in chapter 1, this second, less-known, yet still Nietzschean mimetic tradition cannot be confined to luminous Apollonian (mimetic) representations that set up a transparent mirror to the world. Instead, it includes darker, Dionysian (mimetic) impersonations, identification, psychic doubling, not to speak of the shadows and simulacra endowed with a power of *repetition* without proper origins that generates (mimetic) phantoms nonetheless.

Mimetic appearances of this improper sort of repetition with a difference are numerous in Conrad's shady fictions, and Miller is careful to outline them. For instance, they find a manifestation in Miller's narrative attention to the "echoing episodes" (68) in *Lord Jim* in which the narrative, he writes, calls "attention to the way one episode repeats another" (68). This narrative echo, or repetition, in turn, generates a chain of simulacra that do not rest on a transcendental origin or model, yet generate doubling narrative effects in which "'only differences resemble one another' ['*seules les différences se ressemblent*']" (*Fiction* 5)—as Miller suggests, echoing Deleuze, echoing Derrida, echoing Nietzsche, echoing . . . a chain of exemplary figures that have been tracing these mimetic phantoms since the beginning of aesthetic theory. Alternatively, and pointing to an interplay between linguistic doublings and psychic doubles, in his chapter on the "The Secret Sharer," titled "Conrad's Secret," Miller writes that readers who are annoyed with Conrad's insistence on the mimetic trope of the double "have not seen how the story *mimes* the story's central theme" (148; my emphasis), generating a series of doubling speech acts that reveal a mimetic, unconscious communication central to the tale: namely, that "The narrator often feels he is outside of himself and dwelling inside the skin or inside the sleeping suit of the other man" (144). The shadow-line dividing self from other, inside and outside, "original" and "phantom," Miller subtly indicates, may not be as stable as it appears from the outside.

Further, and perhaps more revealing of how deep mimetic principles inform Miller's rhetorical method of reading, we find traces of *mimēsis* in Miller's superb reading of the famous moon/halo metaphor in "Heart of Darkness Revisited" (76–83)—in my view, one of the most sophisticated close readings to ever have been performed on Conrad's tale. These traces become visible if we realize that they repeat the same mimetic principles we have just outlined—with a difference. In fact, the ontological foundations of the "phantasmal likeness" (77) or *Gleichnis* at play in the spectral doubling of the parable of the moonshine are indicated by its "twice-reflected light" (80). This light, in other words, is twice-removed from that original source of illumination that, already for Plato, was the sun and the intelligible world of ideal Forms it represents in that founding text for mimetic theory which is the *Republic*. And yet, *with* Nietzsche, *contra* Plato, Miller inverses the idealist ontology on which this mimetic image rests. How? By endowing this artistic light far removed from the ideal (Platonic) model with an illuminating power to make us see and feel the darkness all around, a power that despite, or rather because of, its inversion continues to rest on the interplay of two (ancient/Romantic) models of mimesis: namely, mimesis understood as both a reflecting mirror and as an illuminating lamp, generating an interplay between "the mirror and the lamp" (to echo M.H. Abrams—one of Miller's most formidable opponents) on which the "critic as host" brilliantly plays—for future readers to replay.

For those readers, then, given that deconstruction has often been accused of remaining confined within the boundaries of the text, I find it important to echo Miller's insistence that reading, as he understands it, cannot be dissociated from the referential world that surrounds us and, for the moment, still sustains it. There are a number of indications in Miller's text that point in that direction, especially in the second part of the volume where his concerns with ethics become center stage. They are far from having lost their mirroring power to urge critics and theorists to reflect critically on the present and future. For instance, in his detailed reading of the role community, or better, its absence, plays in the shaping of the material vision Conrad dramatizes in *Nostromo*, Miller opens a parenthesis that makes the mirroring, yet not necessarily transparently realistic, link between text and context visible, as he writes: "It is hard to read *Nostromo* and not to think of the long sad history, before and after Conrad wrote that novel, of United States intervention in South America, or even of our recent intervention, governed as it has been by 'material interests,' in Iraq and Afghanistan" (185). And thinking of the "George W. Bush Administration," but with the power to foresee future administrations that cast a shadow on western democracies, he adds: "Running the United States as if it were a corporation was a wonderful opportunity for plunder, trillions of dollars taken from American citizens rather than the mere billions Enron purloined from stockholders. Conrad's Holroyd prophetically anticipates those more recent devotees of 'material interests' and imperial power" (185).

Lastly, in a doubling of Conrad's prophetic insights, the critic as theorist brings out a twice-refracted insight that continues to cast light on the darkness that surrounds us and is now visible outside the text (*hors-texte*) for all to see. In an incisive (implicit) reply to critics like Achebe who encouraged us to consider whether we should read *Heart of Darkness* due to its nineteenth-century ethnocentric bias, Miller acknowledges these racist and sexist linguistic figures as constitutive of Conrad's rhetoric, but, in a forward-looking gesture, also reminds us that "Each must read from himself and herself and testify anew" (89).

In his testimony, then, Miller recognizes that Conrad's description of Kurtz as a "dark shadow" or "ghost" represents the horrors of racism and imperialism in Africa, and at the same time, in a mirroring move that does not entail any contradiction, also *"strikingly anticipates the fascist or violent authoritarian possibilities within capitalist imperialism"* (119; my emphasis). Now that in the wake of January 6, 2021, these possibilities have been made manifest, the forward-looking power of Miller's (anti)-mimetic insight stands at least partially revealed. In fact, this is not a straightforward mimetic reflection that depends on all-too present authoritarian referents; it emerges from the words on the page Conrad uses to make us see. And yet, at the same time, they are endowed with powerful mimetic insights on the (will) to power of a "leader" "'on the popular side'" who could "electrify" the masses (Conrad 72), generating echoes that encourage new readers of Conrad to continue to reflect critically, and thus theoretically, on a voice that seems indeed "to lead into the *heart of an immense darkness*" (77).

These are just some preliminary insights into the mirroring reflections reading *Reading Conrad* can potentially perform. There would be many others. From readers who approach Conrad for the very first time to scholars who have read, taught, and reread these narratives, from the students who need a clear and solid introduction to literary theory in action to the theorists who look back to giants of the past in order to develop new critical and theoretical principles for the future, J. Hillis Miller's *Reading Conrad* provides an admirable place to start—not an origin but a *Stoßpunkt* to develop new readings of our own. In the end, Miller taught us that no one can do our reading for us. My doubling title, "Rereading *Reading Conrad*," was simply meant as a performative encouragement to follow the traces of an exemplary reader that will continue to serve as a model for future generations of readers to come.

ACKNOWLEDGMENTS

This review essay is part of a project that has received funding from the European Research Council (ERC) under the European Union's Horizon 2020 research and innovation program (Grant Agreement no. 716181: *Homo Mimeticus: Theory and Criticism*). For more information, visit www.homomimeticus.eu.

NOTES

1. For a recent interview in which J. Hillis Miller discusses his career-long engagement with rhetorical reading and its engagement from schools that go from New Criticism to phenomenology, deconstruction to the ethical and digital turn, see Lawtoo and Miller, "The Critic and the Mime."

2. Elsewhere, Miller aligns his method to the kind of "reading *lento* that Friedrich Nietzsche advocates": "'When I picture to myself a perfect reader,' says Nietzsche, 'I always picture a monster of courage and curiosity, also something supple, cunning, cautious, a born adventurer and discoverer'" (qtd. in Miller, "How to Read," 255).

3. I pursue this metaphysical line of inquiry in the company of J. Hillis Miller, Philippe Lacoue-Labarthe, and Adriana Cavarero in Lawtoo, *Conrad's Shadow*, part 3.

WORKS CITED

Cohen, Tom, Claire Colebrook, and J. Hillis Miller. *Twilight of the Anthropocene Idols*. Open Humanities Press, 2016.

Conrad, Joseph. *Heart of Darkness*, 5th ed., edited by Paul B. Armstrong, W.W. Norton, 2017.

Deleuze, Gilles. *Logique du sens*. Les Éditions de Minuit, 1969.

Lawtoo, Nidesh. *Conrad's Shadow: Catastrophe, Mimesis, Theory*. Michigan State University Press, 2016.

Lawtoo, Nidesh, and J. Hillis Miller. "The Critic and the Mime: J. Hillis Miller in Dialogue with Nidesh Lawtoo." *Minnesota Review*, vol. 95, 2020, pp. 93–119.

Miller, Hillis, J. "The Critic as Host," *Critical Inquiry*, vol. 3, no. 3, 1977, pp. 439–47.

——. *Fiction and Repetition: Seven English Novels*. Basil Blackwell, 1982.

——. "How to Read Literature." *The J. Hillis Miller Reader*, edited by Julian Wolfreys, Stanford University Press, 2005, pp. 251–58.

Nietzsche, Friedrich. *On the Genealogy of Morals*. Translated by Douglas Smith, Oxford University Press, 1996.

NIDESH LAWTOO
KU Leuven

Contributors

AN NING is Associate Professor at Shantou University, China. She is the author of *The Affirmation of Ordinary Life: A Comparative Study of Middlemarch and Honglou Meng* (2015), and the translator of *Joseph Conrad: A Literary Life* (2017), *The Selected Letters of Joseph Conrad* (2019), *The Selected Essays of Joseph Conrad* (2020), *The Nigger of "The Narcissus"* (2021), and *Heart of Darkness* (2022). Her current research project is entitled *Joseph Conrad: Chinese Perspectives*.

NIDESH LAWTOO is Assistant Professor of Philosophy and English at KU Leuven, as well as Principal Investigator of the European Research Council-funded project, *Homo Mimeticus*. He is the editor of Conrad's *Heart of Darkness and Contemporary Thought* (2012), and the author of three books that rethink the problematic of mimesis in light of contemporary challenges: *The Phantom of the Ego: Modernism and the Mimetic Unconscious* (2013); *Conrad's Shadow: Catastrophe, Mimesis, Theory* (2016; Adam Gillon Award 2018); and *(New) Fascism: Contagion, Myth, Community* (2019). His next book is titled *Violence and the Unconscious: Catharsis to Mimesis*.

JAKOB LOTHE is Professor Emeritus of English Literature at the University of Oslo. His books include *Conrad's Narrative Method* and *Narrative in Fiction and Film* (both from Oxford University Press), and he is co-editor of four volumes in the "Theory and Interpretation of Narrative" series published by The Ohio State University Press. He was elected to the American Philosophical Society in 2018.

JOHN G. PETERS, a University Distinguished Research Professor at the University of North Texas, is past president of the Joseph Conrad Society of America and current editor of *Conradiana*. His books include *Joseph Conrad's Critical Reception* (Cambridge 2013), *The Cambridge Introduction to Joseph Conrad* (2006), *Conrad and Impressionism* (Cambridge 2001), and the Norton Critical Edition of Conrad's *The Secret Sharer and Other Stories* (2015). His articles have appeared in such journals as *Philosophy and Literature, College*

Literature, Studies in the Novel, Studies in Short Fiction, and *English Language Notes.* He has also translated the Japanese poet Takamura Kōtarō's book *The Chieko Poems* (Green Integer, 2007).

BYRON SANTANGELO is Professor of English at Indiana University. He is the author of *Different Shades of Green: African Literature, Environmental Justice, and Political Ecology* (2014), *African Fiction and Joseph Conrad: Reading Postcolonial Intertextuality* (2005), and numerous articles and book chapters in African literary studies, the environmental humanities, and Conrad studies.

ERIK ROBB THOMPSON is Professor of English at the Catholic University of Korea. His areas of interest are Wallace Stevens and Joseph Conrad. His articles have appeared in South Korean journals such as *Mirae Journal of English Language and Literature, The New Korean Journal of English Language and Literature,* and *Modern British and American Language and Literature.*

TUNG-AN WEI received her PhD from the University of Maryland in May 2021. She is an adjunct assistant professor in the Department of Foreign Languages and Literature at National Yang Ming Chiao Tung University in Taiwan. Her article on Conrad's "The Tale" is forthcoming from *The Conradian.* She is working on Conrad's Malay fiction.

CONRADIANA
A Journal of Joseph Conrad Studies

John G. Peters, Editor
Jana M. Giles, Managing Editor
Justin Jones, Assistant Editor
Editorial Interns: Anna Bounds, Kyle Hutchinson,
Melissa Jackson, Jacob Lewis, Angel Szeto

Conradiana, an international journal devoted to and welcoming essays on all aspects and periods of the life and works of Joseph Conrad, is published three times yearly in the spring, summer, and fall.

If possible, essays should cite Conrad's works within the text. Essays must cite a major authoritative edition of Conrad's works (such as the Cambridge Edition of the Works of Joseph Conrad; the Uniform edition of the Collected Works of Joseph Conrad [Doubleday or Dent edition]; or the most recent editions of the Modern Library, Broadview, Norton Critical, Oxford, or Penguin editions of Conrad's works), as approved by the General Editor of *Conradiana*.

Submissions should be double-spaced throughout and follow the *MLA Manual of Style*. Manuscripts may be submitted electronically (preferred) as a Microsoft Word file (or in a compatible format) to John G. Peters, Editor, at jgpeters@unt.edu. Authors preferring to submit a hard copy may do so by sending their work to the Editor at 1155 Union Circle, #311307, Department of English, University of North Texas, Denton, TX 76203-5017.

Correspondence should be directed to the Editor, except in the case of subscriptions and other business matters, which should be addressed to Texas Tech University Press sales office, Lubbock, TX 79409-1037. Books for review should be sent to Ellen Burton Harrington, Book Review Editor, Department of English, University of South Alabama, 5991 USA Drive, N., Room 240, Mobile, AL 36688 (eharrington@southalabama.edu).

Subscriptions are $64.00 for individuals and $120.00 for institutions.

Conradiana is indexed in *Abstracts in English Studies, American Humanities Index, Index to Book Reviews in the Humanities, MLA International Bibliography,* and *Twentieth-Century Literature*.

COVER: Detail from "Joseph Conrad Listening to Music," etching by Walter Tittle, courtesy of the Rare Book Room, Southwest Collection/Special Collections Library, Texas Tech University.

This journal is a member of CELJ, the Council of Editors of Learned Journals.

Conradiana—ISSN 0010-6356
Winter 2018, Volume 50, Number 3
(published three times a year)
Texas Tech University
Copyright © 2018 Texas Tech University Press
Box 41037
Lubbock, Texas

www.ingramcontent.com/pod-product-compliance
Lightning Source LLC
Chambersburg PA
CBHW020947090426
42736CB00010B/1300